L'ARCH
7401 S
B.C. V
Canada

MW00651749

The Jossey-Bass Nonprofit and Public Management Series also includes

Leader to Leader: Enduring Lessons on Leadership from the Drucker Foundation's Award-Winning Journal, *Frances Hesselbein, Paul M. Cohen, Editors*

The Jossey-Bass Guide to Strategic Communications for Nonprofits, *Kathy Bonk, Henry Griggs, Emily Tynes*

Philanthropy and Law in Asia: A Comparative Study of the Nonprofit Legal Systems in Ten Asia Pacific Societies, *Thomas Silk, Editor*

The Power of Character: Prominent Americans Talk About Life, Family, Work, Values, and More, *Michael S. Josephson, Wes Hanson, Editors*

True to Ourselves: A Celebration of Women Making a Difference, *Nancy M. Neuman, Editor*

The Drucker Foundation Self-Assessment Tool for Nonprofit Organizations, Revised Edition, *The Peter F. Drucker Foundation for Nonprofit Management*

Forging Nonprofit Alliances, *Jane Arsenault*

Saving Money in Nonprofit Organizations: More Than 100 Money-Saving Ideas, Tips, and Strategies for Reducing Expenses Without Cutting Your Budget, *Gregory J. Dabel*

Achieving Excellence in Fund Raising, *Henry A. Rosso and Associates*

Sustaining Innovation, *Paul Light*

Boards That Make a Difference: A New Design for Leadership in Nonprofit and Public Organizations, Second Edition, *John Carver*

The Budget-Building Book for Nonprofits, *Murray Dropkin, Bill LaTouche*

Changing by Design: A Practical Approach to Leading Innovation in Nonprofit Organizations, *Douglas C. Eadie*

Powered by Coalition: The Story of INDEPENDENT SECTOR, *Brian O'Connell*

Fund Raisers: Their Careers, Stories, Concerns, and Accomplishments, *Margaret A. Duronio, Eugene R. Tempel*

Winning Grants Step By Step: Support Centers of America's Complete Workbook for Planning, Developing, and Writing Successful Proposals, *Mim Carlson*

Human Resource Management for Public and Nonprofit Organizations, *Joan E. Pynes*

In Search of America's Best Nonprofits, *Richard Steckel, Jennifer Lehman,*

Leading Without Power: Finding Hope in Serving Community, *Max De Pree*

Marketing Nonprofit Programs and Services, *Douglas B. Herron*

Museum Strategy and Marketing, *Neil Kotler, Philip Kotler*

TRANSFORMING
FUNDRAISING

TRANSFORMING FUNDRAISING

A Practical Guide to Evaluating

and Strengthening Fundraising

to Grow with Change

JUDITH E. NICHOLS

Jossey-Bass Publishers • San Francisco

Copyright © 1999 by Jossey-Bass Inc., Publishers, 350 Sansome Street, San Francisco, California 94104.

All rights reserved. No part of this publication may be reproduced, stored in a retrieval system, or transmitted, in any form or by any means, electronic, mechanical, photocopying, recording, or otherwise, without the prior written permission of the publisher.

Jossey-Bass books and products are available through most bookstores. To contact Jossey-Bass directly, call (888) 378–2537, fax to (800) 605–2665, or visit our website at www.josseybass.com.

Substantial discounts on bulk quantities of Jossey-Bass books are available to corporations, professional associations, and other organizations. For details and discount information, contact the special sales department at Jossey-Bass.

This book is printed on paper containing a minimum of 10 percent postconsumer waste and manufactured in the United States of America.

Library of Congress Cataloging-in-Publication Data

Nichols, Judith E.
    Transforming fundraising : a practical guide to evaluating and strengthening fundraising to grow with change / Judith E. Nichols.
—1st ed.
    p. cm.—(The Jossey-Bass nonprofit and public management series)
    Includes index.
    ISBN 0-7879-4495-5
    1. Fund raising.   2. Nonprofit organizations.   I. Title.
II. Series.
    HG177.N48   1999
    658.15'224—dc21

                                                                98-51243

PB Printing   10 9 8 7 6 5 4 3 2 1   FIRST EDITION

The Jossey-Bass
Nonprofit and Public Management Series

Contents

Introduction: How Development Assessment
Can Dramatically Increase Fundraising Results   xi

The Author   xiii

Part One: Understanding the Development Assessment Process

1. What Development Assessment Is and When You Need It   3

2. How to Conduct a Development Assessment: Key Components   11

Part Two: Understanding Your Fundraising Environment

3. Fundraising in a Changing World   23

4. Understanding the Demographic and Philanthropic Trends
That Drive Fundraising   27

5. Realigning Fundraising Strategies to Grow with Change   43

Part Three: Gathering the Information You Need

6. Where to Look: Resources for Environmental Scanning   51

7. Sample Forms for Surveying, Data Collection, and
Information Recording   63

Part Four: The Development Assessment in Action

8. How One Organization Used Development Assessment to
Strengthen Fundraising Programs: A Case Example   101

Index   173

To my family, without whose support

none of my work would be possible

With a special thank you to Jim Greenfield,

Wesley Lindahl, and Martha Taylor, who read the

initial manuscript. Their thoughtful suggestions

and recommendations made this a better book.

Introduction

How Development Assessment Can Dramatically Increase Fundraising Results

THE GOAL of *Transforming Fundraising* is to provide you with the tools you need to analyze how to dramatically increase fundraising results, thereby improving your not-for-profit organization's ability to better serve society through its mission.

This book provides a workbook guide for not-for-profit organizations. It shows how they can conduct, on their own, an assessment of their current fundraising, using internal staff to coordinate the effort rather than an outside professional. Although there are many good reasons for hiring a consultant to conduct a development assessment (most notable among them the sad reality that we are rarely seen as prophets in our own backyards), *Transforming Fundraising* has been written with the assumption that your organization has decided *not* to take that path.

In the early 1980s, when I was just beginning to understand the science of fundraising, I was offered my first opportunity to fully direct a development program. Now *I* was in charge, not only of running the various fundraising components but also of deciding how much of the staff, budget, and other resources should be put into annual giving, major giving, and planned giving campaigns, corporate and foundation relations, and so forth.

Making those decisions forced me to look both backward and forward. What was the fundraising history of this organization? Had that fundraising lived up to its potential? What could the future be like? What would it take to get the organization there? And how did each of the individual parts of the development program contribute to the whole?

Trying to make sense of it all, I checked fundraising publications and books and asked colleagues for their help. Then, not finding a format that fully addressed my needs, I began to develop a tool of my own. I created a format that enabled me to evaluate the organization's current situation and assess its fundraising potential, so that I could realistically identify the strategy steps and tools I needed to get the organization from one point to another as quickly and as cost effectively as possible.

I began calling this format the Development Assessment Process. Since 1981, I have used my assessment process with every organization for which I have worked, either as staff or as a consultant. The Development Assessment Process has been tested in educational, health, human service, fine and performing arts, and community-based organizations. It has been successfully used as an evaluation tool by such not-for-profits as the American Quarter Horse Foundation (animals), American Lung Association (health), Camphill Foundation (disabilities), Mercy Corps (international aid), Oregon Symphony (arts), Salvation Army (human services), and Wayne State University (education). Girl Scouts of the USA bought a version for use with all 314 of its councils. Often I hear back from not-for-profits who undertook the process that—years later—the Development Assessment Process remains a valid tool for assessing their progress toward fundraising goals.

Recognizing that few of us have the luxury of stopping our day-to-day responsibilities as we step back to analyze our organizations, *Transforming Fundraising* is focused and succinct. Chapters are short and to the point, guiding you from the generalities to the specifics quickly and decisively.

Part One, "Understanding the Development Assessment Process," provides background information to help you decide whether you need and want to undertake an assessment. In Chapter One, I review the rationale for doing a fundraising assessment, discussing why and when to conduct the assessment and how the Development Assessment Process maximizes fund development efforts. Chapter Two then explains how the assessment process is organized, with sections to help you identify the key players, assemble the assessment components, and create the plan of work.

Part Two describes how to analyze the ways outside influences are affecting your fundraising. In Chapter Three the general concepts underlying the understanding and acceptance of change are explained, and Chapter Four focuses on the current philanthropic and demographic trends and explains how the latter affect the former. Chapter Five reviews methods for fundraising and examines how changes in your audiences might affect the way you go about raising money.

Part Three offers tools for information gathering. Chapter Six recommends resources for environmental scanning, and Chapter Seven contains a sample assessment survey for collecting the historical information and outside materials needed to evaluate a not-for-profit's past performance and future capabilities in fundraising.

Transforming Fundraising concludes in Part Four, Chapter Eight, with a sample assessment report, which puts all these elements together.

The Author

JUDITH E. NICHOLS is a development consultant with not-for-profit clients across the United States, Canada, the United Kingdom, South America, Australia, and Europe. A popular trainer and presenter, she specializes in helping organizations understand the implications of changing demographics and psychographics on fundraising, marketing, and membership.

Nichols has been a featured speaker and trainer at numerous conferences, workshops, and symposia around the world. Her books include *Lessons from Abroad: Fresh Ideas from Fund-Raising Experts in the United Kingdom; Global Demographics: Fund Raising for a New World; Growing from Good to Great: Positioning Your Fund Raising Efforts for BIG Gains; Pinpointing Affluence: Increasing Your Share of Major Donor Dollars; Targeted Fund Raising: Defining and Refining Your Development Strategy; Changing Demographics: Fund Raising in the 1990s;* and *By the Numbers: Using Demographics and Psychographics for Business Growth in the 1990s.* Nichols's books are included in the Heritage Collection of the National Society of Fund Raising Executives (NSFRE).

Nichols is editor of the newsletter *New Directions in Philanthropy* and previously was editor of the newsletter *Philanthropy Trends That Count.* A columnist for *Contributions* and a member of the international editorial board for the *Journal of Nonprofit and Voluntary Sector Marketing,* she has also had numerous articles published in *Fund Raising Management,* the *NonProfit Times, Advancing Philanthropy, Girl Scout Leader, YMCA Perspective, Professional Fundraiser* (UK), and *American Demographics.* She has been interviewed by such publications as the *Chronicle of Philanthropy, Canadian Front and Centre,* and the *Irish Times.*

Nichols has more than twenty-five years of fundraising and marketing experience, working with higher education, arts and cultural, health, human benefit and social service, membership, and youth organizations. Her clients include the American Cancer Society, American Heart Association, American Lung Association, American Quarter Horse Foundation, Girl Scouts of the USA, Mercy Corps International, National Society for the Prevention of Cruelty to Children (UK), Presbyterian Church Foundation (USA), Royal National Lifeboat Institute (UK), The Salvation Army, and Volunteers of America. She is an advisory board member for the International Fund Raising Workshop, held each year in the Netherlands.

A certified fundraiser (CFRE), Nichols served as vice president for development at Portland State University, Oregon, and headed development efforts at Wayne State University in Detroit and at the New Jersey Institute of Technology. While she was at Wayne State, her development program received the silver medal for Most Improved Development Program of the Decade from the Council for the Advancement and Support of Education. An active member of the National Society of Fund Raising Executives, she has served on both the Michigan and Oregon NSFRE boards. She holds a Ph.D. degree in business management from California Coast University.

TRANSFORMING
FUNDRAISING

Part One

Understanding the Development Assessment Process

Chapter 1

What Development Assessment Is and When You Need It

A WELL-DONE DEVELOPMENT ASSESSMENT can evaluate dispassionately an organization's ability to meet both its current and its future goals and objectives. The assessment process outlined in this book looks at organizational mission, the commitment of the board of trustees, audiences that support the organization, and the fundraising infrastructure before tackling overall development strategy and specific fundraising methodologies. Always, the goal is to provide pragmatic recommendations that can be logically incorporated into current operations.

What Is the Role of a Development Assessment?

The Development Assessment Process creates an opportunity for free and open dialogue among an organization's internal and external audiences. The process encourages thoughtful feedback about these areas of concern:

- Where are we today and what are we offering to the public, to our donors?

- Is what we are today what we want to be tomorrow?

- Does our potential public perceive us in the same manner we perceive ourselves?

- Does it, by and large, approve of our work and endorse our current objectives? Does it understand our goals and objectives for the future?

- What kinds of financial resources will we need to finance the objectives we have in mind for tomorrow?

- What are our financial priorities in everything from facilities construction to program funds?

- Are the people in our organization behind the vision and do they understand the goals ahead?

- With whom are we competing for funds? Is there anything unique or distinctive about our approach to our field?

- How do we best communicate our distinctions, goals, and objectives to our public?

- Where do our board members and volunteers fit in?

- How do the roles of the executive director, associate directors, board members, development and other staff, and volunteers complement each other in the development process?

Even though not-for-profits regularly set fundraising goals, too often they do not take the time to measure the progress of their development programs, or they evaluate these programs on the wrong criteria. As a result, staff, gatekeepers (including the executive director and the voluntary leadership), and other stakeholders (including donors, volunteers, and clients) may be disappointed with the results. Even worse, people in the organization may think they are doing a good job in raising funds when a much greater potential could have been realized.

Max De Pree, chairman emeritus of Herman Miller, Inc., and a member of the board of the Peter F. Drucker Foundation for Nonprofit Management, cautions us that in his "experience a failure to make a conscious decision about what it is we're going to measure often causes discombobulation and a lack of effectiveness and a lack of achievement. We're good at talking about what we think about some things, and sometimes we're good at talking about what we believe, and we're often good at talking about what our goals are to be. When it comes time in nonprofit groups to measure, we're not nearly as specific as we ought to be" (*Leading Without Power*, 1997, p. 47). This critique is often true of our development programs.

Once the assessment with its specific measures is completed, its findings are not the end of the process; rather, they become the basis for opening up dialogue among board members, among staff members, and between board and staff members, often moving both formal and informal organizational gatekeepers to a new level of understanding, cooperation, and participation.

The formal report document can help an organization's gatekeepers (both staff and the voluntary leadership) understand their roles in managing change. Usually a series of meetings or retreats is held. Through the assessment process—the gathering of information, the formal report preparation, and the debriefings—the following questions are asked and answered:

- How genuine are our development needs?

- How committed is our board to achieving development success?

- Do we have a constituency base that is able and willing to respond to those needs?

- Do we have the resources needed to carry out our development objectives successfully?

- How competent and prepared are our staff and volunteers?

When Does Conducting a Development Assessment Make Most Sense?

Just as a not-for-profit organization should conduct overall strategic planning every few years, it should carry out development assessments on a regular basis to help everyone involved understand both the history and the potential of the fundraising program. A full review should be done every three to five years.

Although there's never a wrong time to step back from your day-to-day activities and look at the larger picture, there are some particular moments that might trigger a need for a development assessment. It is especially helpful to get "out of the box" when

- The organization needs to hire a new development officer and wants a clear understanding of what can be accomplished in fundraising, how it can best be done, and what the costs and the time commitments will be to do it.

- The development officer is new to the organization and, before plunging into the day-to-day fundraising, wants all parties to have a clear understanding of what can be accomplished in fundraising, how it can best be done, and what the costs and the time commitments will be to do it.

- The organization has reached a plateau in its current fundraising efforts and wants to move to the next level of achievement; before this can happen, all parties need a clear understanding of what can be accomplished in fundraising, how it can best be done, and what the costs and the time commitments will be to do it.

- The organization has reached the end of a strategic planning cycle that resulted in recommendations for several new programs; before launching the new programs or launching into another planning cycle, it wants to assess the current programs.

- Those associated with the organization believe that the current fundraising is far from its potential capacity, and they want to conduct an assessment to analyze the areas of potential.

- The organization has several development divisions within a larger development office; the larger development office will not undertake a complete assessment for some time but wants to assess the programs in one area of responsibility.

- The organization has a new executive director, or CEO, who is urging different fundraising programs; before the board and staff make decisions to change programs, the organization conducts an assessment to evaluate what is currently working well.

- The organization's funding from sources such as government and United Way is shifting, and the leadership wants an assessment to identify new sources to make up for potential shortfalls.

What a Development Assessment Does

By opening up a dialogue among key players and structuring information gathering for more accurate decision making, the Development Assessment Process encourages staff and volunteers to take an active role in development planning. The assessment provides a pragmatic analysis of the organization's development strategy. The objective is to gather unbiased information. The goal is to dramatically increase fundraising results.

A development assessment can take as little as four weeks to complete, but twelve weeks is a more realistic timeline—especially if this is your first attempt. During this period you prepare the personalized assessment survey, gather the information using the survey, review the materials, and hold on-site meetings (both one-on-one and in groups) and telephone meetings with key staff, volunteers, donors, and members of the community who are involved in the program or influential in the community. Once the background materials have been gathered and evaluated and the necessary interviews held, a written analysis is prepared. The analysis defines the key areas of concern, the roles of volunteers and staff, and the priorities for implementation and recommends a timeline for achievement within the context of realistic, yet challenging, goal setting.

In addition to analyzing the fundraising strategy, the assessment should review and recommend needed infrastructural steps and examine image building, public relations, donor constituency relations, community outreach, and fundraising, sponsorship, and promotional opportunities if relevant.

Again, the goal is to provide specific recommendations that can be logically incorporated into current operations.

A development assessment helps your organization maximize its fund development efforts in three major ways:

- It evaluates what the organization is currently doing and what competition the organization faces in generating financial support.

- It realistically assesses the organization's potential for generating financial support from different audiences.

- It suggests strategic steps and tools to solicit financial support cost effectively from the identified target audiences.

What a Development Assessment Does Not Do

The development assessment focuses on fundraising. It does not do a thorough management analysis of the not-for-profit, nor does it do a study on the actual function of the service(s) the organization delivers. It will measure public perception and donor perception of the function and management of the organization as well as internal perception of the fundraising operation.

Many development assessments are conducted by consultants. This is often the case in larger organizations such as colleges and universities, where the process involves a number of fundraising departments and requires a commitment of time that a staff person cannot give. Sometimes it might be politically advisable to use an outsider—for example, if the head of fundraising is leaving and the assessment recommendations are needed in looking for a replacement, or if the director of development is suspected to be the problem.

But, especially if your not-for-profit is smaller, has a tight budget, or has strong leadership, conducting the assessment yourself can be extremely satisfactory. Once an organization is committed to this internal approach, it must determine who will guide the effort. Although input from numerous parties is vital, one individual must be in charge and ultimately have the responsibility for making—and defending—the assessment's recommendations.

The Role of the Assessment Coordinator

Chances are that you will serve as the *assessment coordinator*. Typically, the assessment coordinator is the staff person in charge of fundraising at the organization. The coordinator will most likely have the title of director of development, director of fund development, development coordinator, or director of fundraising or a variation on these titles. If a not-for-profit does not have a paid staff position devoted to fundraising, the assessment coordinator should be the individual who currently has the responsibility for coordinating fund development efforts. In many smaller or grassroots charities, this person will be the executive director. Occasionally this person will be a volunteer.

The assessment coordinator is responsible for preparing and conducting the development assessment survey. The responsibilities include all the elements mentioned earlier:

- Collecting the requested internal data
- Seeking out the necessary demographic data
- Conducting one-on-one interviews with key staff, board members, volunteers, donors, and members
- Facilitating focus group meetings with key members of the greater community
- Reviewing and analyzing the written materials gathered for the survey
- Reviewing and analyzing the input from participants in the interviews and focus groups
- Creating the written report
- Facilitating board and staff meetings and retreats to conduct a dialogue about the assessment's findings
- Carrying out the specific recommendations of the report
- Preparing ongoing evaluations of progress toward development goals and objectives

In addition to these functions, the assessment coordinator must create a preliminary consensus about the assessment itself. Of all the functions assigned to the assessment coordinator, this is the most important. Both formal and informal gatekeepers play a crucial part in the Development Assessment Process by providing insights on current and proposed strategies. *It is strongly recommended that you do not begin an assessment without making sure that the executive director and the board understand what you are planning to do and agree on its importance.*

Conducting a development assessment requires a major commitment of time and energy. Unless the organization's leadership truly buys in to the process and is willing to accept the trade-offs involved (for example, the assessment coordinator will have to limit other activities while the assessment is underway), there is a strong possibility that the coordinator will find himself or herself caught between responsibilities. For that reason, it is imperative that gatekeepers have true understanding and full buy-in.

Soliciting Input

It is especially important that there be a full and open dialogue from the start of the process. The executive director and board chair, or president, must let all members of the organizational family know the purpose of the development assessment and must provide the assessment coordinator with their strong endorsement. Unless the staff and volunteers understand why the assessment is being done and how the process works, they are unlikely to see the necessity for considering the assessment an organizational priority.

Moreover, in the course of conducting the assessment the coordinator may bring up unpleasant history and require the organization to face issues that have been ignored by silent consent. Without the willingness of staff, board and other key volunteers, members, donors, and people from the greater community to provide honest and full input and feedback, a development assessment cannot succeed.

The executive director and board chair should inform their constituencies of the possibility that an assessment will be undertaken as soon as the coordinator begins to explore that possibility. Once the organization decides to go forward with the process, it is strongly recommended that the decision to proceed with the development assessment be put in a memo and distributed to all staff and all board members and other volunteers.

It is equally important that the assessment coordinator be viewed as a *team player.* As the coordinator gathers information, he or she must be sensitive to the time constraints of all the different assessment participants. In Chapter Two, I review a typical timeline. The timeline the coordinator intends to follow must be plotted out carefully and shared with those the coordinator wishes to involve well in advance of scheduling specific appointments. Invitations to meetings and focus groups must be sent out early. Follow-up must be done promptly.

Chapter 2

How to Conduct a Development Assessment: Key Components

THE DEVELOPMENT ASSESSMENT is first and foremost a process of information gathering. The assessment's findings and recommendations are based on

- The answers given on the assessment survey

- A review of the internal and external compiled data

- The comments received during one-on-one and focus group meetings with members of the board, key volunteers, community leaders, members, donors, and staff

The more information you have, the better you will be able to understand what should and could change in your fundraising. The main vehicle for collecting background information is the assessment survey. Once that information has been collected and analyzed, the development assessment's key tool is a written report that explains the findings and makes pragmatic recommendations.

A development assessment provides an opportunity for holding retreats or meetings for the board and staff at which assessment findings are discussed and the actual work begins toward the goals and objectives. A retreat or meeting also serves as a training event. It has three components:

1. A debriefing on the development assessment findings

2. An explanation of what is required for the organization to move forward

3. Specific next steps for volunteers and staff

Finally, a development assessment provides the development director and those with the responsibilities for implementation with an ongoing process of feedback that keeps the specifics of the development plan on track.

This chapter describes in more detail the assessment survey, the interviews for the survey, and the assessment report.

The Assessment Survey

The assessment survey compiles the development and related history of an organization. (A sample survey appears in Chapter Seven.) It encourages an organization to be objective about its past and current fundraising. To be useful, the survey must be thoroughly and thoughtfully completed. One of the purposes of the survey is to provide a starting point for evaluating and refining the current development strategy. You carefully analyze the not-for-profit's organizational and fundraising history by gathering as much historical data as possible *before* you recommend any changes.

The assessment survey enables an organization to make a directed, step-by-step analysis of the development program. It looks at both direct fundraising and related areas of leadership, vision, and mission and the organization's public relations and image.

The survey's main areas are organized as follows:

- *General background:* relevant demographic, economic, social, and philanthropic indicators in the local community and appropriate regional and national trends

- *Organizational background:* organizational structure including mission and vision; organizational stability; anticipated short-and long-term operating, capital, and endowment needs; and staff and volunteer leadership

- *Fundraising background:* history of each program and methodology, including dollars raised, costs, donor acquisition and retention, strategy, and materials

The Interviews

Whereas the assessment survey concentrates on gathering historical facts and figures, interviews and meetings gather *narratives* about an organization. The goal is to get a sense of the organization from both internal audiences (those who know the organization intimately—the staff, board and other volunteers, clients or members, and donors) and external audiences (those who do not know the organization intimately but who are persons of influence and affluence in the greater community).

The development assessment survey and interviews will generate a considerable quantity of paper to be collected, evaluated, and reviewed. The sample assessment survey in Chapter Seven includes sample forms the coordinator can use to collect information efficiently.

Internal Audiences

The meetings and appointments with internal people gather information on

- How internal people perceive the *culture* of the organization
- How internal people work together and share information
- What monies are needed and why

All meetings, internal and external, are scheduled to enable fact finding. The participants should be encouraged to give candid answers that will draw an accurate profile of the organization. Taken together, the interviews enable the assessment coordinator to see the whole picture. In conversations with stakeholders, the coordinator covers vision, mission, and organizational perceptions that affect development. How well do those within the organization communicate, coordinate, and collaborate? The coordinator also asks for development specifics: What are we raising money for? How have these goals and objectives been set?

Whom do you interview? As many individuals as you can within your time limitations! The main concern here is buy-in: Have those associated with and concerned about the organization had a chance to express themselves—both positively and negatively—about its history and its future? It is always better to flatter by including too many people than to offend by asking too few.

Interviews with the following internal audiences are *required:* the chair of the board, the executive director of the organization, and the development office staff.

In addition, it is strongly recommended that the coordinator interview the program directors and program staff, current and past board members and committee chairs, current and past volunteers, major individual donors and corporate and foundation funders, and also selected clients and members. The sample survey in Chapter Seven includes specific questions for the director of development, executive director, and program directors to answer, as well as questions about board member effectiveness.

The number of individuals who could be involved can be overwhelming. One-on-one interviews can take from fifteen minutes to (more usually) one hour. Meetings with the executive director and board chair often go longer, two hours or more. In the interests of saving time, the coordinator may interview certain people in group meetings. Often an open invitation to program staff for one meeting and an invitation to all but the key members of the board for another meeting will suffice. Typically, an organization employing up to two hundred individuals will need to put aside a week for the internal one-on-one and group appointments. Ask those you interview to recommend others to interview as well. Remember, you're looking for both the informal and formal gatekeepers.

A one- to two-day block of time needs to be scheduled with the development staff—the director and the professional and support staff—unless it's a one-person shop. If the assessment coordinator *is* the shop, put the same amount of time aside to conduct this full interview with yourself, both asking and answering the questions. This time is used to look over the development systems and strategies in depth. The purpose is to review and expand on the answers the assessment survey has collected about how specific fundraising methodologies are handled.

External Audiences

The external focus appointments gather information on

- How external people perceive the organization vis-à-vis other not-for-profits serving the community, state, nation, and world
- How effective the organization's outreach and the communication of its image are to people of influence and affluence
- What insights external people have about resources not usually available to the organization

The opinions of key members of the community not currently involved with the not-for-profit balance the opinions of those close to it. The coordinator should include representatives from community banking, financial, educational, medical, military, legal, and agricultural institutions and also people representing cultural, religious, and political institutions. In addition, it is useful to obtain the opinions of representatives of the philanthropic community, such as representatives of United Way, local community foundations, and other not-for-profits serving audiences similar to yours.

A good way to gather input from those not involved with the not-for-profit is a focus group. Focus groups serve a unique function by bringing the organization face-to-face with the market—the real world—it seeks to involve. They provide a rapid means for gathering information in the actual language people use to describe their thoughts, ideas, and behavior. A focus group may also serve as a first step in identifying influential community members' interest in working with the organization as key volunteers.

A focus group meeting of people with influence in the community can provide insights on how these community leaders perceive the organization. However, because these are busy individuals and often have not been involved with your organization, you might have to extend the invitation to a large number of community leaders to gather a group of six to twelve on a specific date. Also choose a central location with a relaxed atmosphere for the meeting, ideally a conference room. The meeting should take no more than one and a quarter hours.

Identify all the individuals who would be ideal board members. Once you've chosen the guest list and decided on the time and place (ideally, a nonmeal time so the meeting purpose remains clear), extend invitations. Make an advance phone call in which you confirm each person's availability or ask them to suggest another person to interview in their place. Follow that call with a formal invitation, signed by the board chair and sent three weeks before the event. Each invitee who agrees to attend is sent a confirming letter and a handout packet consisting of a letter of thanks from the board chair, the organization's mission statement, and a short brochure or fact sheet covering the organization's clients, programs, and services.

At the meeting the board chair welcomes the group members, reminding them that the purpose of the meeting is to obtain their feedback on what they perceive to be community needs and the role that the organization is playing and could play. Next the executive director spends five to ten minutes explaining the organization's vision. Both the board chair and executive director remain available to participate. Then the facilitator (usually the assessment coordinator) poses appropriate questions: for example, "When I say, 'type of organization,' what do you respond (youth, medical, educational, and so forth)?" and, "When I say, 'ABC Organization,' what do you respond?"

Depending on the size of your community and the availability of key participants, you may want to schedule more than one focus group. And for those not available for group meetings, offer to meet one-on-one.

The Written Development Assessment Report

The written report is prepared based on a review of the compiled internal and external materials (the survey findings) and the outcomes of the meetings with members of the board, key volunteers and members, donors, staff, and community leaders. (A sample report appears in Chapter Eight.)

An assessment report must be personalized to acknowledge the individuality of an organization for which it is prepared. However, each assessment report typically follows this general format:

Introduction

Executive Summary

Developing the Case for Support

- Does ABC Have Credibility with the Public?
- Is There a Rationale for Raising More Private Dollars?
  - Defining the Need
  - Interpreting the Need in Dollars
- Can ABC Attract Increased Private Support?
  - Defining the Positive Indicators
  - Defining the Concerns

Moving to the New Paradigm

- Addressing Organizational Issues
- Strengthening Board Leadership in Development
  - Helping Board Members Understand Responsibilities
  - Setting and Approving Development Goals and Objectives
  - Developing Gift Stewardship and Accountability Guidelines
  - Determining the Fundraising Role of the Executive Director
- Reorganizing the Development Office
  - Computerizing
  - Making the Budget Commitment
  - Evaluating Current and Future Fundraising Methodologies
  - Evaluating Fundraising Staff

The Proposed Development Strategy

- Moving from a Broad-Based to a Focused Development Strategy
- Increasing Community Understanding of ABC
- Increasing Results by Strengthening the Individual Fundraising Components

- Major Giving

- Planned Giving

- Annual Giving

- Special Events

- Corporate and Foundation Relations

Recommended Steps for Implementation: Timeline

Resources: Supporting Materials

- Resource A: Responsibilities of the Board (Sample Job Description)

- Resource B: Sample Gift Stewardship and Accountability Guidelines

Appendixes

- Appendix A: Program and Service Needs Assessment Results

- Appendix B: List of Participants

- Appendix C: List of Materials Requested and Gathered

- Appendix D: Copy of the Development Assessment Survey

The introduction outlines the purpose of the assessment. This is boilerplate, and you will be able to use much of the introduction provided in the sample report.

The executive summary gives the key findings of the assessment in summary form. This is often the piece of the report that is used at the debriefing meetings with members of the board and staff.

In "Developing the Case for Support," general background information is provided. This section explains, in detail, the fund development *climate*, describing what is happening nationally and locally and how the organization is perceived by current and potential funding constituencies. This section summarizes the strengths and the areas of concern that affect an organization's ability to successfully generate financial support, and it states the rationale, or *case*, for support and how much support is needed.

"Moving to the New Paradigm" provides the big picture. Here the coordinator looks at how well positioned the organization is to carry out its current or revised development strategy. Is the organization supportive? Does the board understand its role? Is the development office properly staffed and equipped? This section might also look at any organizational areas that influence fund development, for example, memberships, programs, and product sales.

"The Proposed Development Strategy" is the heart of the report, articulating very specifically how the organization's fundraising might best be organized. Within its pages, this section discusses how best to define development objectives, both in narrative and in dollar amounts. It provides clear, realistic recommendations for moving the organization's development program forward. It contains an analysis of all aspects of the organization's current development efforts, and this analysis includes all facets of a full development strategy.

In "Recommended Steps for Implementation," the assessment report tackles the need to move things along. The timeline presented in this section enables an organization to continuously evaluate whether it remains on target as it implements the development plan.

The "Resources: Supporting Materials" section contains, as needed, detailed explanations of concepts. I have found typically that material on the responsibilities of the board and sample guidelines for gift stewardship and accountability are needed. (Examples of these materials are included in the case study report in Chapter Eight.) Other materials that might be needed are sample job descriptions, explanations of specific fundraising programs, and samples of materials used successfully elsewhere.

Appendixes relating to the way the survey was conducted and to key survey data are typically included at the end of each development assessment report for easy reference. Usually they include lists of the people who were involved in the survey and of the materials that were gathered as well as a copy of the survey itself.

The Development Debriefings

Once the written development assessment report has been created, a series of debriefings is essential for ensuring that gatekeepers who are involved in the day-to-day fund development activities or whose duties and responsibilities affect fundraising understand the philosophy underlying the findings of the development assessment and will proactively contribute to reaching the assessment report's goals and objectives.

Plan on separate debriefings for the executive director and board chair, the key program staff leadership, the board of trustees, and the development staff. Depending on the size and complexity of the organization, other debriefings might be necessary as well. *Do not attempt to skip this step or to condense the debriefings!* Unless everyone associated with the development effort, formally or informally, is helped to understand what is being proposed and why it is being proposed, the necessary changes will *not* occur.

Typically, three areas are discussed at a debriefing:

- How is our organization positioned for fundraising? (Explore the organization's slice of the funding pie as realistically as possible.)

- What is the role of organizational staff? Of members of the board? Of development staff? (Explore the commitment each person must make and his or her role as an advocate for the organization.)

- How do we move ahead? (Explore the strategy for fundraising and the part organizational staff, board members, and development staff each must play.)

Debriefings need not be long: forty-five minutes to one hour might suffice for those people least involved with the actual development functions. However, key players need to sense the importance of what is being proposed and be given the time to ask their questions. For most boards (or their executive committees) this will require two and one-half to three hours. Development office staff should be debriefed in an all-day retreat.

The Plan of Work

As mentioned earlier, twelve weeks is a realistic amount of time for conducting a development assessment. Gathering information through the assessment survey and external sources, scheduling and holding appointments and focus groups, reviewing the gathered materials, and preparing the written report should take ten weeks. The key debriefings should be scheduled to begin immediately after the report is presented to the CEO and board chair—within two weeks of assessment completion is ideal.

Here is a sample overall timeline for the Development Assessment Process:

Day 1	Confirmation of development assessment; identification of assessment coordinator
Weeks 1–4	Appointment scheduling and collection of survey information
Week 4	Initial review of survey information
Weeks 5–6	Interview appointments with organizational leadership and staff, board members, donors, and community leaders
Weeks 7–8	Preparation of outline or draft of written report
Week 8	Short debriefing meeting with executive director
Week 9	Preparation of full written report
Week 10	Full debriefing meeting with executive director and chair of board to review full written report
Week 12	Debriefing meetings with organizational staff, the board, and development staff

After the Assessment Is Conducted

Without a leadership commitment to implement the findings of the development assessment, the work on the survey, the on-site analysis, and the written report will prove an empty exercise. The objective of the Assessment Development Process is to provide logical, doable steps that will enable an organization to reach agreed-upon fund development goals within a specific period of time. Therefore it is of absolute importance that the timeline and recommendations articulated in the report be followed closely. As implementation goes forward, the day-to-day tasks become the responsibility of the assessment coordinator. However, the board and organizational leadership cannot sit back. They must be committed to working as a team. Specific dates for quarterly evaluations of progress toward goals and objectives should be agreed to.

Part Two

Understanding Your Fundraising Environment

Chapter 3

Fundraising in a Changing World

WHEN THINGS REMAIN STATIC or change slowly, a reluctance to assess how well or poorly its fundraising is going may not put a not-for-profit severely at risk. But the environment today is one of hyperchange: in today's tumultuous times, many organizations find themselves needing to be constantly *in transition.*

To thrive, not merely survive, charities cannot assume that their traditional methods for fundraising will continue to work. Many are facing major changes in their funding partners and scenarios. Not-for-profits need a tool to identify what the next stage should—and could—be.

Once you understand a not-for-profit's development history, you can decide on a logical fundraising plan for the future. As Edward Cornish, president of the Futurist Society, notes, watching trends helps us automatically begin to correct our conception of current realities so that it is more up to date ("Using the Future to See the Present," *The Futurist,* July–Aug. 1997, p. 4).

The Changing Nature of Change

It used to be that our environment changed in fairly slow increments, allowing us to take our time in adjusting. But, that's no longer true. Back when mankind was in its infancy, major changes to the social, economic, and demographic environment might occur once a millennium. But now the time frame for major change has speeded up dramatically. We've moved from once-in-a-thousand-years changes to once-in-a-century changes to once-in-a-decade changes to changes that happen faster than we can assimilate them. In fact, the one indisputable fact in a sea of change is that change is both inevitable and nonnegotiable! From now on, we will *always* be in transition.

Change of any kind is disruptive. The constancy and speed of change causes most individuals and organizations problems, because, even though change can be transforming, revitalizing, and a source of energy, too often we view change negatively, as threatening, disruptive, and anxiety provoking.

When their environment changes dramatically, people tend to react predictably. Initially, they exhibit patterns similar to those associated with grieving:

1. They feel awkward, ill at ease.

2. They feel loss; they mourn.

3. They feel alone, isolated.

4. They feel overwhelmed.

Different individuals exhibit different levels of readiness in accepting changes. Once they begin to accept the changes, they worry about having enough resources. And, because change is unsettling, if the pressure is taken off, most will revert to their old behaviors!

Joel Barker, a futurist who has cautioned us over and over again about the danger of not recognizing when change is occurring, warns that when the rules change fundamentally, we must shift paradigms or face death!

> A revolution is coming!
>
> Will you
> ☺ Lead it?
> ☺ Follow it?
> ☹ Sleep through it?
>
> [Adapted from Karl Albrecht, *The Northbound Train*, 1994, p. 13.]

In fact, the best time to change your paradigm is when the old one is still working—then you have time to try out new options. Karl Albrecht (*The Northbound Train*, 1994, p. 13) notes that "the time to start thinking about the meaning and direction of the business is not when things start going to hell but well in advance of the shock wave. Any business whose leaders do not have a clear sense of where the environment is going and what kind of a future the business must prepare for may be risking its actual survival."

Unfortunately, too often, individuals and organizations become complacent and ignore the realities of change all around them. New paradigms tend to show up sooner than they are wanted. Because our old paradigm makes it hard for us to see new paradigms, we try to ignore inevitable change—until it's too late.

Environmental Scanning

There are several options for dealing with change: some proactive, many reactive. The sad truth is that—too often—change takes not-for-profits unaware. Then they play catch-up, trying desperately to move to the new reality. Disasters happen when they fail to learn, they fail to anticipate, and they fail to adapt.

To prevent an organization from operating in a vacuum, its leaders must understand today's environment. You can use environmental scanning to help your organization to

- Capitalize on early fund development opportunities, rather than lose these opportunities to the competition

- Receive early signals of impending problems that can be defused if recognized well in advance

- Sensitize volunteers and staff to the changing needs of the organization's constituencies

- Access a base of objective, qualitative information about the organization's service area that can be used in planning and that will stimulate thinking

- Improve the organization's image with its public by showing that it is sensitive to community needs and responsive to such needs

- Provide a means of continuing, broad-based education for the organization's management team

In scanning the environment, there are two key general questions to answer:

- What are the relevant demographic trends?

- What are the relevant philanthropic trends?

Only by understanding the implications of this vital information can you realistically determine how well positioned your organization is in each key area and then confidently restructure your development program to maximize your organization's share of private support. The sample assessment survey in Chapter Seven contains questions that will help you get a good start on both external and internal environmental scanning. Chapter Four provides demographic information that suggests many viewpoints from which to assess your donors and programs.

Once you have scanned the national, regional, and local demographic and philanthropic environments, you must gather internal information to gain an understanding of what is happening demographically and philanthropically within your organization.

In order to answer the question, Who should our future donors be? you must be able to answer questions about current donors: What are the donor demographics, including age, gender, income, education, profession, ethnic or racial background, religion, life stage (single or married, children or not), and dwelling location (urban versus rural versus suburban)? What are the donor psychographics (values, attitudes, lifestyles)?

And you must objectively review the historical results of fund development: How successful has your organization been when success is viewed as a function of income by type of campaign or by fundraising methodology? When it is viewed as a function of expense to income raised? How well has the organization done in keeping donors and finding new prospects? Overall, what are the results compared to the goals set?

Douglas C. Edie (*Changing by Design*, 1997, p. 10) asserts that "the question is not whether a nonprofit organization will change but how it will go about the job of changing." Once an organization acknowledges the need to change its fundraising, it must find the best way of accomplishing the task of changing. Using both the external and internal information you have diligently assembled, you will be able to decide the answers to two key questions:

- Who are the best prospects?

- What are the best strategies?

As you analyze both the external and internal information, you will be able to

- Objectively evaluate what the organization is doing to raise money

- Realistically assess the potential for raising money from different audiences

- Confidently suggest strategy steps and tools to get from where you are to where you need to be quickly and cost effectively

Chapter 4

Understanding the Demographic and Philanthropic Trends That Drive Fundraising

IN ORDER TO CHOOSE the most relevant development strategies for your not-for-profit, you must first look at what is happening in a broader context.

Reviewing National Philanthropic Trends

There are at least three national philanthropic trends that fundraisers must understand:

1. *Personal philanthropy in the United States has been flat for over twenty-five years.* Overwhelmingly, philanthropic contributions come from individuals. According to *Giving USA 1998: The Annual Report on Philanthropy for the Year 1997* (American Association of Fund-Raising Counsel, 1988), historically, individuals have been the largest source of charitable contributions. Through both willed and lifetime gifts, individuals have been responsible for 85.0 percent to 90.2 percent of giving over the past three decades. Foundations have been responsible for between 5.2 percent and 9.3 percent of contributions, and corporations between 4.0 percent and 6.3 percent.

In 1997, for example, personal giving reached $109.26 billion (out of an estimated $143.46 billion) and represented 76.2 percent of total giving. Bequest giving reached $12.63 billion and represented 8.8 percent of giving. Together, giving by living individuals and by their estates amounted to $121.89 billion, which was 85 percent of total 1997 contributions.

In 1965, Americans contributed just over $35 billion a year to charity; by 1997, charitable giving had grown to $143.86 billion. Although the increase appears impressive, when total contributions to churches, charities, and other institutions are adjusted for inflation they are not nearly as impressive. In inflation-adjusted dollars, charitable giving from 1985 to 1997 actually is down nearly 12 percent. From 1985 to 1997, even the three-fourths of contributions to organizations that go to religious institutions have not kept up with inflation, declining 1 percent in real terms. And with the exception of annual gifts to educational institutions, which are up 84 percent in adjusted dollars over the same 1985–1997 period, the average U.S. household is giving much less to other charities (down 44 percent) and political organizations (down 65 percent).

A second measure of charitability evaluates annual giving as a percentage of the gross domestic product (GDP). Consistently in the United States, charitable contributions remain fixed from 1965 through 1998 at just 2 percent of the GDP. Both the lack of upward movement and the small percentage are troublesome, suggesting that—for all the means employed by the philanthropic sector—Americans do not consider giving a priority. The wealth of Americans has increased greatly, but their private philanthropy has reflected neither their concerns for their society nor their available wealth.

Finally, in relation to their total household incomes, most Americans give away only a small percentage of their money. The Barna Research Group notes that 75 percent of adults gave less than $500 to not-for-profit organizations, including churches, in 1995. Only 25 percent said they had given $500 or more to all types of not-for-profits—churches and other charities—combined in 1995. Of that group, only 10 percent donated upward of $1,000 for the entire year to all not-for-profits combined, and just 3 percent gave away $3,000 or more.

2. *Foundations and corporations are saturated with requests for their dollars.* Too often, rather than creating solid relationships with their most logical funders, many charities are going for the numbers. For example, 70 percent of all foundations are found in the New York metro area. The vast majority of their grants go to organizations serving the New York metro area. Thanks to the computer, it is now possible to send out "personalized" grant proposals to hundreds of potential funders with a keystroke. Too many charities flood an unresponsive marketplace as a result.

Although most not-for-profits prefer unrestricted and undesignated donations, foundations and corporations today are indicating they view themselves as *seeding* innovative programs that demonstrate cooperation among not-for-profits in the community, rather than providing ongoing support for a particular organization's established programs and services. Corporations and foundations are creating partnerships to focus on key social issues, such as public education and housing. If this trend continues, there will be an obvious, increasing drain on funding for all social programs that have traditionally received support.

Foundations are also looking seriously at giving more operating dollars to a few key organizations instead of spreading their dollars out with little impact in any one area.

And family foundations are now being taken over by a completely new generation, with new ideas of funding priorities and many times lacking loyalty to the local city where their families' wealth originated.

When an organization finds itself one of the small group of corporations' favored charities, that corporate support often comes with strings. Increasingly, the growth in corporate philanthropic funding is not a growth in charitable dollars but in marketing dollars. When corporate philanthropic dollars are available, corporations are becoming more focused on defining the partnerships they will support. A number of major corporate sponsors are evaluating their support from a return-on-investment orientation. They look to quantify this return on investment in terms of increased customer or employee participation. For providers of human services, such program impacts are not easily measured.

3. *The urgency of the need for charitable dollars is ever increasing.* As government and the private sector look at new ways to solve social problems and fund the basics of quality of life in the United States, new not-for-profits have sprung up in response to human needs. Americans have voted to have more functions returned to the private sector and to have nongovernment agencies deliver more government services.

In 1946, there were approximately 100,000 not-for-profits. By 1963, the sector had grown to over 500,000. Today, the pot of charitable giving is divided among nearly 1.4 million exempt organizations—roughly 940,000 more than thirty-eight years ago—which account for half of all U.S. hospitals, half of all colleges and universities, almost all symphony orchestras, 60 percent of social service agencies, and most civic organizations. If we add in membership and professional organizations, the number of exempt organizations in this country rises to nearly 4 million. In the next decade, this multitude of not-for-profits must reinvent the paradigm of competition to move to a collaborative model, with greater use of private-public and private-private partnerships. The sample survey in Chapter Seven includes questions that encourage a close look at other not-for-profits as competitors but also as potential partners.

Reviewing U.S. Demographic Trends

Increasingly, not-for-profits' ability to raise private monies is influenced by what is happening not just locally but also regionally, nationally, and internationally. Thus, before you can assess how well your not-for-profit is doing, you must become familiar with the *outside parameters,* as they influence how effectively your organization can position itself for fundraising. You must understand what is happening that is beyond the control of your organization.

Because the vast majority of fundraising dollars is contributed by individuals, it makes sense to begin by looking at what is happening to these individuals in a context broader than philanthropy. It's important to understand that donors will begin to consider charitable giving only once they have addressed the major concerns in their own lives. The reality is that fundraisers do not drive the process of giving—they only facilitate it. I begin every workshop I do by asking fundraisers this question: "Do you really think your donors and prospects wake up with the first thing on their minds being, 'I feel philanthropic'?" It is unlikely that the answer will be yes. It is important that those responsible for fundraising understand what's happening in society in regard to populations, technology and communication, and financial styles. Only with that understanding can they begin to offer hypotheses on why and when donors and prospects will give.

The prospects and donors of today and in the foreseeable future are already determined: only those who have already been born or who are most likely to be born can be solicited to fund the missions of charities and not-for-profits. Demographically, these donors and prospects are dealing with increasing longevity and represent an increasing diversity. Using information provided by the U.S. Bureau of the Census, we can summarize as follows:

Increasing Longevity

More Americans are simply living longer. At the turn of the century, Americans' average longevity was just forty years of age. Today, the average American lives to be seventy-nine years old if female; seventy-two years old if male. But these statistics are misleading because they take into account everyone who dies *before* the age of sixty-five. If instead we ask how much longer the individual who reaches sixty-five has to live, a very different picture emerges, because for every year a person lives after age sixty-five, longevity lengthens out dramatically. In fact, many individuals who reach sixty-five will live an additional thirty years or more!

We are beginning to hear on a regular basis of individuals living past the century mark. A recent story in the press told of a woman in France who, on her eighty-second birthday, sold a future interest in her apartment to a young man of 40. He died at 80; she outlived him, dying in 1997 at the age of 122. No wonder Willard Scott of *Good Morning America* has stopped wishing happy birthday to anyone under one hundred years of age!

Because it takes fifteen to twenty years for our perceptions to catch up with reality, many individuals haven't quite yet understood that they may live as many adult years after age sixty-five as before it. Once they do realize it, traditional major giving—the sacrificial gift of one-half to one-third of one's assets usually made in one's sixties or seventies—may be viewed as financially irresponsible, even among the small group of the truly philanthropic. In fact, ethically, development officers may have an obligation to caution prospects that planned gifts and bequests make more sense than sacrificial gifts made during the donor's life. The window of opportunity for the traditional major gift is closing; by the close of the century, few if any donors will be willing to put themselves at risk.

In addition, the members of the huge baby boom population (those born between 1946 and 1964) are in their middle age. By the year 2002, the majority of U.S. adults will be over the age of fifty. From the 1960s through the 1980s, fundraisers depended on boomer audiences for acquisition of new donors and prospects. As they age, however, boomer donors are likely to have decided their charitable priorities. Busters, the following adult cohort (also known as Generation X, and born between 1965 and 1977), are considerably fewer in number.

As a result, the proportions of the U.S. population (and in fact of the population in every developed nation) are shifting. In 1989, thanks to the aging of the seventy-six million–plus baby boomers, a majority of U.S. adults were over the age of forty. Between 1990 and the year 2020, the under-fifty population is projected to grow by only 1 percent, but the fifty-plus population is projected to grow by 76 percent.

And increasingly, because women live an average of seven years longer than men, the elderly will be female. Women outnumber men by nearly three to one past the age of eighty-five. Because of their longevity, 86 percent of the wealth of this country passes through hands of women. Although women are more charitably inclined than are men (making three times the number of charitable gifts), they are more cautious financially and demonstrate a different set of charitable priorities as well.

Increasing Diversity

Fundraisers must be aware of at least four aspects of diversity in the United States:

1. *Not-for-profits are dealing with an increasingly culturally and ethnically diverse base of prospects.* By the year 2010, one out of every three children will be either nonwhite or Hispanic. Not-for-profits need to learn how to be inclusive in their client populations, volunteers, boards, and donors.

Hispanics: The Emerging Majority

It is estimated that only thirty years from now, Hispanics will surpass blacks as the largest minority group in the United States. By the year 2020, the U.S.

population will include forty-seven million Hispanics, and within a century, Hispanics could constitute up to 30 percent of the U.S. population, approximately ninety-nine million people. Half of all Hispanic Americans live in California and Texas; when New York and Florida are added, these four states contain more than two out of every three Hispanics living in the United States.

However, being Hispanic in the United States means different things depending on where you live. In New York, the background of the dominant Hispanic group is Puerto Rican; in Texas, California, and other parts of the Southwest, it's Mexican; in Florida, it's Cuban. Other Hispanics have their roots in the Dominican Republic, Colombia and other Latin American countries, or Spain.

Despite their differences, Hispanics have a bond, based primarily on language (Spanish) and also on some cultural characteristics: between 80 percent and 90 percent of Hispanics are Roman Catholics; they are extremely loyal to both people and organizations; they place great emphasis on the importance of higher education; they are outer directed, looking for signals of acceptance by society; and they are very family and community oriented. Much of their philanthropy is directed back to the communities they or a previous generation of their family left.

Asian Americans: Growing Exponentially

Spurred by the 2.4 million Asian immigrants who arrived in the United States during the 1980s, there has been an 80 percent increase in the number of Asian Americans. They are the fastest-growing minority group in the United States. The number of Asian Americans (including Pacific Islanders) grew from 3.8 million in 1980 to an estimated 6.9 million in 1989 and onward to 8 million in 1991.

Asian Americans are geographically clustered. There are thirty-eight metropolitan areas with Asian populations of at least nine thousand, and these areas are home to about 75 percent of all Asian Americans. The greatest concentration is on the West Coast (fully 56 percent of Asian Americans live there, compared to 21 percent of all Americans), except for Asian-Indian Americans, who are concentrated in the Northeast. Nearly four out of ten Asian Americans (39 percent) live in California, and about one out of ten (11 percent) lives in Hawaii. Twelve states (California, Hawaii, New York, Illinois, New Jersey, Texas, Massachusetts, Pennsylvania, Virginia, Florida, Michigan, and Washington) have over one hundred thousand Asian Americans, five times more than in 1980.

Asian Americans are the most highly educated of all ethnic populations. In 1990, 77.5 percent of all Asian and Pacific Islander Americans aged twenty-five and over were at least high school graduates, when the national rate was 75.2 percent. In addition, 36.6 percent of Asian and Pacific Islander Americans were college graduates, compared to 20.3 percent of the total U.S. population.

Despite their enormous range of differences in language, social class, and national history, Asian Americans share many cultural tendencies. These include strong loyalty to family, community, and work; modesty and reserve; a reluctance to complain or express emotions directly and a dislike of confrontation; respect and obedience to authority; sensitivity to the attitudes of others; and a strong work ethic. Many of their contributions are directed to family and the community.

Black Americans: The Largest Minority

Today's black population is twenty-seven million, or 12 percent of the U.S. population. It is growing at a rate nearly three times faster than the white population.

Like Hispanics and Asian Americans, blacks are clustered geographically. Six metropolitan areas have black populations greater than five hundred thousand (Washington, D.C., Philadelphia, Detroit, Atlanta, Baltimore, and Houston), and three have populations over one million (New York, Chicago, and Los Angeles-Long Beach).

Despite the enormous diversity among African Americans, sociologists have attributed several cultural tendencies to this group: directness and spontaneity, expressiveness, sense of community, and a great regard for family and religion. Pepper Miller ("The African-American Mindset: Community Growth and Change," *The Market Segment Report*, Spring 1992), president of a Chicago-based research firm, notes that African Americans in general yearn for a sense of acceptance and belonging and are therefore very image conscious. Blacks want to be accepted by mainstream society, not singled out. Their contributions, as a percentage of income, outstrip those of non-Hispanic whites.

2. *As individuals' lives lengthen, there will be more differences among age groups.* Their *generational anchors*—key points of reference stemming back to childhood—will not be the same. Their philanthropic personalities and attitudes toward money will not be the same. When they are no longer able to address prospects and donors homogeneously, fundraisers will need to be familiar with the generational anchors of many subgroups of individuals. They will need to be more sensitive to reaching different generations of donors, using appropriate methods of communication and marketing for each cohort. Here are the five age groups with which fundraisers will deal:

- *Depression babies.* The thirty-two million Americans born prior to 1939 have *civic* personalities, believing it is the role of the citizen to fit into society and make it better. Always remindful of the lessons of their childhood, they have conservative money personalities.

- *World War II babies.* Born from 1940 to 1945, the individuals in this small group of sixteen million Americans were taught to be *silent*, believing in the will of the group rather than individuality. Their parents drilled the lessons of the Great Depression into these Eisenhower babies, but they reached adulthood in golden economic days, benefiting from real estate appreciation, a booming stock market, portable pensions, government entitlements, and inflation. Now in early retirement, many are willing to spend on themselves if not on charity.

- *Baby boomers.* America's seventy-six million *idealists,* born between 1946 and 1964, have been hard for society to swallow. Taught from birth that they were special, boomers believe in changing the world, not in changing to fit the world. Having always lived in a society of inflation and having no memories of the Depression, they have a different understanding of money. They tend to buy first and pay later and to like monthly payment plans and using credit cards. Although Depression and World War II Americans tend to believe that an annual gift of $25 is a meaningful amount, boomers and younger adults believe it takes at least $100 to make a difference. Baby boomer donors give generously—they are giving in record numbers, percentages, and amounts. Martha Taylor, vice president at the University of Madison Foundation, notes, for example, that "for higher education, a $1,000 annual gift is a normal 'ask' for a baby boomer at most major educational institutions" (personal communication, 1998).

- *Baby busters.* The thirty-three million *reactive* Americans born between 1965 and 1977 are the first generation of Americans to distrust the American Dream. They don't believe life will be better for them than it was for their parents, and they see their role in life as pragmatic. Often called Generation X, they want to fix rather than change. Still being supported in adulthood by parents, many have high discretionary incomes they will give to charities they work with. Highly computer literate, busters prefer the cashless society.

- *Baby boomlets.* The seventy-two million *civic* children of boomers, born from 1978 through 1994, hold many of the values of an earlier generation. They are growing up in a world without boundaries and are likely to extend their philanthropy well past their own country. Because idealistic parents are often willing to be guided by their children, the young children in educated and affluent families are a key to some of the changing charitable funding priorities of the boomer cohort.

In addition, both Depression and World War II babies tend to be cash payers, distrusting newer technologies. They tend to listen to society's recommendations and like to support traditional charities, including United Way. Conversely, midlife and younger Americans (boomers, busters, and boomlets) are likely to look for *personal* charities and to dislike workplace giving. More participatory in personality, they tend to support only organizations they actively work with.

3. *Women have greater potential for major donations in their own right.* Almost half of the wealth of this country is already owned by women, and as described earlier, 86 percent of the wealth in the United States passes through women's hands. Of the 3.3 million Americans classified as top wealth holders (annual reported incomes of $500,000 or more) by the Internal Revenue Service in 1986, fully 41.2 percent were women. By 1992, 43 percent of individuals with assets of $500,000 or more were women. Women also make up 35 percent of the country's fifty-one million shareholders.

Increasing numbers of women are earning more. Although only 6 percent of those earning $50,000 or more in 1980 were women, by 1986 that figure had doubled to 12 percent. Many of the higher-earning women are single or married without children and have higher disposable incomes. (The higher a woman's educational attainment, the fewer births she has had or expects to have. It also is more likely that she plans to have no children. For example, some 20 percent of women with five or more years of college do not plan to have children, compared to only 7 percent of women who have not completed high school.) And as today's senior (male) executives retire, 50 percent of the next group of managers are women.

Entrepreneurial boomer women are growing their own businesses in record numbers. In 1990, women started companies at three times the rate of men. More than five million women today lead small to medium-sized growth businesses, including businesses with the potential to become top companies of the future. Women entrepreneurs are often motivated differently from men entrepreneurs: according to an Avon report, female entrepreneurs are more likely to be concerned with issues of happiness and self-fulfillment (38 percent), achievement and challenge (30 percent), and helping others (20 percent) than with monetary rewards (12 percent) (*Inc.*, April 1990).

There are more unmarried and never-married midlife women than ever before. There are fewer unmarried men (37.6 million) than unmarried women (44.3

million) in the United States, reports the U.S. Bureau of the Census. The number of women aged thirty-five to fifty-four who live alone is likely to increase from 2.6 million in 1990 to 3.4 million in 2000. That's a 30 percent rise among women in their boomer years, compared to a 24 percent rise for all women living alone. And when marriage occurs, often children do not. There is a trend toward later marriages and reduced child bearing. In 1960, 72 percent of women aged twenty to twenty-four were married. Today, 61 percent are not. The drop among those having babies is greater yet. Fifty-four percent of women aged twenty to twenty-four were mothers thirty years ago; now just 28 percent are. And among high-achieving women, 60 percent of executive women have no children, compared to 3 percent of their male counterparts. Older women are increasingly single. There are fourteen million single women older than fifty-five, compared to only four million single men. Moreover, most women marry men older than them-selves. As a result, nearly half of elderly women are widowed, compared with just 14 percent of elderly men. These women control the disposition of their own estates and often those of their spouses as well. Baby boomer women will typically outlive their husbands by at least fifteen years.

The demographic and economic changes in women's lives have been accompanied by a resounding changing in attitudes: women with an earned income are more likely to choose their own philanthropic directions or bring a stronger influence to family philanthropic priorities.

In addition, women tend to save more of their incomes than do men. They are more attuned at an earlier age to concerns about outliving assets, making them prime candidates for planned gifts. Women on their own will represent one in six households through 2001. When the baby boomers start to retire in 2010, that proportion is likely to grow.

Many men and women don't communicate in the same ways. Building rapport, listening well, and personalizing are keys when cultivating and soliciting women donors. Be especially careful not to use peer pressure: although men respond well to the challenge of one-upmanship, it is usu-ally ineffective with women. Here are some additional keys to understand-ing communication differences:

Content. Men generally talk about money, sports, and business. Women generally talk about people, feelings, and relationships.

Style. Men express to fix. Conversation is a competition. They talk to resolve problems. Women express to understand. They support conversation. They talk to the context.

Structure. Men are precise, to the point, without descriptive details. Women tend to give details.

4. *Finally, not-for-profits need to factor in lifestyle and life stage differences.* A growing number of adults are moving through life at their own pace: postponing or not having children, taking sabbaticals from careers, returning to school, starting new businesses, and so forth. Remarriages, second families, and older relatives who need care produce differences in the ways adults of similar ages look at their ability to be charitable. Rather than assume that individuals move up the traditional *donor pyramid*—graduating from smaller annual gifts to sacrificial major gifts and ultimately to bequests and planned gifts—fundraisers may need to look at the *intersection* of lifestyle and life stage with fundraising methodology: a more holistic approach than that employed to date.

Demographic Trends Drive Fundraising Strategies

Here is a summary of the demographic trends that should be driving not-for-profits' fundraising strategies:

Increasing Longevity

- The population is aging. Proportionally, fewer new adults (for acquisition) are entering the population.

- Americans are living longer and are concerned about outliving their assets.

- Most American adults (42 percent) are currently idealistic middle-aged baby boomers with very different psychographics from the older, civic audience not-for-profits have depended on.

- Woman are making up a larger portion of our older population and thus gaining increasing responsibility for determining the disposition of large amounts of wealth.

Increasing Diversity

- The United States is diversifying ethnically and racially. Members of the white, non-Hispanic audience have traditionally felt welcome as donors and volunteers in traditional not-for-profit organizations, but members of most minority groups have not. Fundraisers must work to change people's perceptions, so all will feel welcome.

- There are five key generations, with differing psychographics and financial lifestyles. Fundraisers need to develop a different communication style for each.

- Lifestyle, not life stage, determines a person's attitude toward philanthropy and the ability to be philanthropic.

Not surprisingly, the trends in population and technology and communication that have dominated the past two decades of business marketing have also shaped overall fundraising in the United States and in turn guided development strategies. Thus the focus of fundraising during the 1980s and early 1990s has been heavily on gift acquisition through direct mail, workplace giving, and special events. During this time, not-for-profits could

- Count on civic donors who responded to the authority and paternalism inherent in workplace giving

- Use direct mail as their primary communication vehicle, because audiences were literate, computers could make each appeal "unique," and mailing costs were relatively inexpensive

- Count on boomers entering adulthood for an ever-increasing audience of energetic younger adults eager to attend events for networking and socialization

Now, as new prospect populations dominate the scene, fundraising methodologies and communication styles must change as well. The one thing we know with certainty about the future is that it's likely to be different from the present. In recent years, there have been disquieting signs that business is not proceeding as usual. As audiences are diversifying, fundraisers need to respect their communication, technology, and use of time preferences. For example,

- Our boomer audiences are now middle-aged and time pressed. Growth in involvement in formal recreational activities (including galas, auctions, and athletic events—especially trekking, tennis, and golf) will not keep pace with growth in population. Attendance at many types of special events is slowing, even dropping.

- Technology has moved rapidly, and different audiences now have different communication preferences. Not only must the message be different, the medium must be as well. Simply increasing the number of blanket appeals is no longer bringing in the desired results. Although the mature donor continues to prefer direct mail, boomers respond better to telephone appeals coupled with an advance letter or video. Busters expect us to communicate via the computer.

As the Population Changes, Charitable Priorities Change

The top charitable recipients in the United States are the donor's own religion, the donor's own schools, the donor's own health care organization or health concerns, and the fine and performing arts the donor attends. In many other countries, including the United Kingdom and Canada, giving is more altruistic. It is directed more heavily at helping people in underdeveloped nations, animals and the environment, and individuals with physical or mental disabilities, and at solving community problems such as homelessness, hunger, and domestic violence.

Much of U.S. charity has always been *self* connected and focused on larger, institutional organizations. In other countries, most of education, the arts, and health care have been heavily subsidized by the government and therefore charitable giving could be directed at larger, more global concerns. In most other industrialized countries, social services, higher education, and assistance with local problems are paid for by the government. Only in the United States is the charitable sector so responsible for so many aspects of social services, education, arts, and health. Thus Americans have directed their charitable giving toward those institutions to which they were connected and in which they knew of a need.

With the advent of the global economy and the availability of the Internet, Americans have begun to shift some support toward organizations serving national and international concerns.

Interestingly, beginning in the 1990s, we've also seen a trend in the United States toward a new public commitment to public and societal benefit, the environment and wildlife, and international relief and development. This suggests a modest, but growing, shift to support of more altruistic and grassroots areas. The changing philanthropic profiles of today's donors may be the reason. The bulk of donors prior to the mid-1990s was made up of individuals born prior to World War II. These mature, civic-minded donors give because "it's the right thing to do." Men civics, especially, give out of loyalty and duty. But some have tended to assume a quid pro quo—that the organizations they support will in turn be useful to their communities or to their families or others they know. Therefore they have concentrated their contributions on *their* religions, *their* colleges and universities, *their* hospitals and health care providers, the human service organizations *their* families might use, and the arts organizations *they* enjoy.

Civics strongly believe in loyalty in the form of *paying back* for benefits they have derived from an organization or community. One reason is that because of World War II, civics don't take anything for granted. The basics of a good community were topsy-turvy during that war. Mature individuals know a time when local churches, arts groups, schools, and health care providers suffered and their neighbors and families suffered as well. They feel grateful for the *basics* of life—a world with no depression, no world war, no shortages. Civics give too from fear of not having these resources for the community, nation, and world.

Their attitude is in contrast to the baby boomers' attitude. Everything has always been there for the boomers. They take the basics of their communities for granted. Boomers grew up in a time of plenty: their fathers went to college, many on the GI Bill; their mothers stayed at home, giving them full attention; the economy boomed. They grew up testing and questioning authority. They wanted accountability and details. Boomers are idealistic. They can afford to be so—the basics of life are provided for. Boomers will not give just because they have a relationship with an organization or have been users or graduates of an institution.

A truly major paradigm shift is occurring as our world is becoming one giant connected entity. Civics' international and national giving also tends to be done through traditional agencies to which they have a personal tie— their church to help the poor overseas, their college to help underprivileged students. Idealistics and reactives are more open to seeking out and choosing charitable partners from every and any corner of the globe. The World Wide Web, e-mail, and faxes make communication from continent to continent as rapid and reliable as from city to city. Electronic fund transfers make payments—whether in dollars, pounds, or guilders—easily flow across the miles, ignoring currency differences.

A New Era for Philanthropy?

I am firmly convinced that the coming century will be one that bodes well for philanthropy in the United States and around the world. As the older generations of donors pass out of the giving arena due to concerns about outliving their assets or to death, the middle-aged boomer generation is moving into its own. Being idealistic by nature, boomers give because "it feels right." Interestingly, baby boomer men align more closely with women of all ages in their attitudes toward giving and patterns of giving than they do with older men. Baby boomer and younger women are strong supporters of social advocacy causes, including environmental protection, abortion rights, and gun control.

Perhaps as a result of their more inner-directed attitudes, many middle-aged Americans are reevaluating their lives. And with so many boomers having postponed marriage or having remarried later in life, record numbers have young children. Boomlet children are the first generation to see the world without boundaries. They view the entire world as their backyard, and their concerns are global. Many affluent boomer parents are influenced when their children query whether the values their parents espouse are being lived. The youthful idealism of boomers appears to be reawakening in community activism and, in a larger sense, in a desire to make the world their children inherit a better place.

Increasingly, surveys conducted by Gallup, Harris, and Roper Starch are showing that Americans believe materialism, greed, and selfishness are dominating U.S. life, crowding out values centered on family, responsibility, and community. People are expressing a strong desire for a greater sense of balance in their lives—not to repudiate material gain but to bring it into proportion with nonmaterial rewards. According to Roper's *Public Pulse* (March 1997), 23 percent of the American population (forty-five million adults) feel personally responsible for the quality of life in their communities and take action to ensure that their communities are sustainable places to live.

Viewing philanthropy not as a duty but as a reward, boomers have already passed their parents' generation as donors. Boomers are 42 percent of the adult population, but they already contribute 47 percent of donations according to a survey done in 1995 by the Russ Reid Organization and Barna Research Group for the Direct Marketing Association ("The Heart of a Donor," January 1995).

I believe that there will be a continued increase in boomer giving and a pronounced shift to giving to the more altruistic charities. In fact, we may already be seeing the first positive signs: U.S. charitable giving began to increase significantly in 1995 and has shown steady increases each year since. Although 1996 and 1997 represent modest increases of just 5 percent each compared to previous years, when these increases are combined with the over 11 percent increase of 1995 over 1994, the total increase does represent the largest jump in percentage since the mid-1980s, as measured in current dollars.

In addition, since the early 1990s, more U.S. individuals than ever before have given to the more global charitable areas: public and society benefit, international aid, and the environment. These areas have demonstrated double-digit gains, although the actual dollars are still small. Indeed, in the past few years it is these organizations that have shown the largest increases in public support. *Giving USA 1998* notes that public and society benefit organizations, including many support organizations, reported growth of 10.8 percent in 1997 and 6.6 percent in 1996. These organizations also reported double-digit growth in 1994 and 1995, years in which overall giving did not grow that fast. Environmental and wildlife charities reported a 7.4 percent increase in 1997 after reporting only 1.5 percent growth in 1996. This fits well with findings that an overwhelming number of Americans consistently put environmental concerns at the top of their priorities, as evidenced in surveys by Gallup and Roper. Likewise, international affairs organizations reported 15.0 percent growth in 1997, after a 4.6 percent decline the previous year.

The opposite pattern was seen in self connected charities. Giving to arts and cultural institutions increased by 9.6 percent in 1996, but these organizations reported a 2.8 percent decline in 1997. Health organizations and hospitals reported a 10.0 percent increase in 1996, but they gained only 1.0 percent in 1997. Over the same two years, religious giving showed a slight decline (6.1 percent compared to 6.6 percent), and human services showed a minute increase (4.1 percent compared to 4.0 percent). Only education runs contrary to the pattern of declining share of support demonstrated by charities that have benefited from donor self-interest: it gained 12.3 percent in 1997, following an 8.8 percent increase in 1996.

Not-for-profits must focus on increasing the total charitable dollars contributed annually by encouraging new leadership from both the wealthy and affluent and by increasing the public-private partnerships for the delivery of education, social services, and health care in this country. In the years ahead, congregations, colleges, hospitals, arts groups, and human service organizations may need to reinvent their communications style to better attract and retain the more idealistic donor of the twenty-first century. For example, endorsements from key individuals in the community (such as board members) do not carry weight with midlife and younger adults. Neither do vague appeals to "do the right thing" or to "pay back" or to "be loyal." One church, for instance, stopped calling its pledge Sunday "Loyalty Sunday" because its new baby boomer supporters didn't respond to that title (Martha Taylor, personal communication, 1998). Fundraisers will need to be more specific about what their organizations are doing, how they are doing it, and the results they have had.

We are seeing a window of opportunity for far-sighted organizations that carefully chart a move to the new paradigms for donors and fundraising as they continue to benefit from the traditional audiences that have served them so well. Although the dollars flowing from individuals into altruistic charities are still modest, the trend toward their increased slice of the giving pie is clear. And with that trend, a warning should be sounding for those traditional organizations that have typically benefited from the U.S. charitable psyche.

Chapter 5

Realigning Fundraising Strategies to Grow with Change

BEFORE STARTING the Development Assessment Process, you should identify your underlying fundraising assumptions, your philosophical framework for the development strategies you will be recommending. This is important because the assessment compares what is happening in a development office with what you say ought to happen.

My development philosophy—based on a combination of my practical fundraising experience and research and the teachings and writings of colleagues—is that fundraising efforts are best focused on individuals rather than corporations and foundations (85 percent of gift giving versus 5.7 percent from corporations and 9.3 percent from foundations in 1997) and that special event fundraising should be recognized as a high-cost, low-loyalty vehicle. My philosophy further assumes that the overall strategic fundraising goals should be as follows:

- Work with your best prospects first.
- Match prospects to methodologies.
- Redefine major giving to include larger annual giving, cumulative giving, and special opportunity gifts.
- Focus on after marketing rather than acquisition.

Work with Your Best Prospects First

Your best prospects are those who are already part of your *family.* Spend the majority of your time and effort with those who are most likely to respond. This is also known as the *70/20/10 percent rule.*

Concentrate 70 percent of your efforts in renewal and upgrading, working first with those who have the greatest stake in your organization. The first group will consist of members of the board: if they don't endorse your efforts by making an early financial commitment, why should members of the greater community? The next group comprises *current* donors, volunteers, members or clients, and staff. A final group within the 70 percent contains *lybnts* (last year but not this year) and *sybnts* (some year but not this year), comprising *former* donors, volunteers, members or clients, and staff.

Then devote 20 percent of your efforts to expansion. On the one hand, your *logical* universe will consist of prospects who are strong demographic or psychographic matches to your current donors. If your average current donor is a married female, you might test lists with similar demographics. If your cause tends to be liberal rather than conservative, look to trade lists with another not-for-profit with similar psychographics. On the other hand, you might want to acquire contributors who exhibit characteristics lacking in your current donor pool. Perhaps you want a more diversified ethnic or racial base so as to better mirror the general community your not-for-profit serves. Or perhaps your typical current donor is elderly, and you would like to acquire donors with an average age of fifty instead of seventy-five.

Finally, reserve just 10 percent of your efforts for wild cards. These are over-the-transom gifts or fantasy major gift prospects. There's no logical reason to expect these gifts to happen, so all you can do is wait for the donors to identify themselves, and then you can do the work required.

Match Prospects with Methodologies

Generally speaking, you want to focus your best fundraising methodologies on your best prospects, moving to the next level of strategy where the breaks make the most sense. This would include moving from visits to telecommunication due to a lack of staff or volunteers; from telecommunications to direct mail because of budget constraints.

- *Major gifts.* Focus on face-to-face appointments for all ages of audience, but recognize that midlife audiences are more receptive to visits for all levels of gifts; because of their idealistic psychographics, they consider anything they do to be special.

- *Midlevel gifts.* Focus on renewal and upgrading and on moving donors to monthly giving. Use telecommunications (linked to a direct-mail preapproach and often incorporating a video) for midlife audiences.

- *Modest gifts.* Use direct mail alone for mature audiences; consider telemarketing, television, and radio for midlife and younger audiences.

Redefine Major Giving

According to both the Independent Sector and the American Association of Fund-Raising Counsel, major gift giving has decreased even as incomes are rising. Although there were over 60,000 millionaires in the United States by 1989 compared to just 4,281 in 1980, there were just 888 gifts of over $1 million in 1989 compared to 418 in 1980. In fact, by the end of the 1980s, in terms of average annual giving, the wealthy were giving 60 percent less than at the beginning of the decade.

The wealthiest Americans—those who earn more than $1 million annually—are decreasing the share of their income that goes to charity. Contributions from the rich have declined from an average of more than 7 percent of their reported after-tax income in 1979 to less than 4 percent in 1990. (The most generous donors may not be the wealthy but rather the poor and the widowed. Independent Sector reported a Gallup Organization study based on 1989 charitable giving that showed that the poorest U.S. households gave 5.5 percent of their income to philanthropic causes, an amount equal to three weeks of their gross pay [*Giving and Volunteering in the United States,* 1990]. Americans earning more than $100,000 donated 2.9 percent of their income, about one and one-half weeks of their earnings. Widows and widowers contributed more of their income [3 percent] than did single, married, or separated people. Middle-income people, earning between $40,000 and $75,000, contributed at about half that rate.)

If the truly major gift is not the logical path for the coming century and the poor cannot provide a greater share of philanthropic dollars, what is the answer?

Pay More Attention to the Middle of the Donor Pyramid

It makes sense to concentrate fundraising efforts on the *affluent market.* To get affluent individuals to give, a not-for-profit needs to change its development strategies so they accommodate affluence rather than only wealth. It needs to define major donors in terms of both size of gift and cumulative giving. After all, if a donor loyally gives to an organization year after year for thirty, forty, fifty, sixty years or more, isn't he or she a major donor? Reaching affluent potential donors is a focus of the case study report in Chapter Eight.

The U.S. Census Bureau defines an *affluent* household as one having at least $50,000 in yearly income. Today, 20.8 of U.S. households meet this standard; 16.6 percent have annual incomes over $60,000. Choosing to target households earning at least $50,000 to $75,000 per year will give a not-for-profit more prospects than it can possibly use. Over nineteen million U.S.

households qualify as affluent under this criterion. Many are more than capable of providing gifts of $1,000 to $10,000 annually. Instead of automatically targeting the small pool of easily identified persons at the pinnacle of wealth in the community, fundraisers should think about focusing on a broader base of affluence.

The affluent market is one of the fastest-growing markets in the United States. Higher productivity, two-income households, lower taxes, more college-educated adults, and lower inflation, among other dramatic developments, have combined to produce this new level of affluence. From 1979 to 1990, the proportion of households earning $50,000 to $74,999 a year rose by about a sixth to 15 percent; the proportion earning $75,000 to $99,999 climbed by a quarter to 5 percent; and the proportion earning more than $100,000 doubled to 4 percent, or four million households. In the past decade, affluence in the United States has increased at a phenomenal rate, enlarging an already undertapped market of potential donors. Since 1980, the number of affluent households has doubled. All indications are that the ranks of the affluent will continue to grow, and the 1990s have been low-inflation years, so the increase in numbers will be genuine.

When you decide to focus on affluent individuals, you should make these two changes in the way you do your fundraising:

1. *Stop thinking of major donors in terms of one-time gifts of assets; instead, ask more often for larger gifts from income.* The average millionaire has a yearly income of only $120,000 to $130,000. And 80 percent of the wealthy are first-generation millionaires, understandably cautious in making sacrificial gifts. Neither they nor the majority of affluent prospects are able—or willing—to strip themselves of assets to make gifts of five figures. Thomas Stanley, author of *Marketing to the Affluent* and *The Millionaire Next Door,* notes in the latter book that an average income of about $120,000 a year is "four or five times what the average family brings in, but it's not megabucks."

So instead of ultimate gifts, think more boldly about annual gifts. Because greatly increasing numbers of Americans are affluent and have significant discretionary income at their disposal, look for prospects who can and will make yearly gifts from $1,000 to $10,000 regularly. Although only 1 percent of individuals number themselves among the upper class, 14 percent are members of upscale households. Look for the members of these more than 19 million households. Furthermore, about 1.5 million households of those 19 million have a net worth of over $1 million. Because affluent households reflect the increasing diversity in U.S. society, donors will be found among all ages, both genders, and all ethnic and racial backgrounds. It's important for fundraisers to have an overall understanding of the demographics and psychographics of these diverse donors that they will come in contact with during the next ten to fifteen years.

2. *Instead of assuming donors move up the giving pyramid linearly, assume that the best times for major gifts will be those times when lifestyle and life stage intersect, providing donors with the ability to do more.* Although major gifts can be made at the end of a donor's life, there are many other times of significant change in individuals' lives. Key life stages include empty nesting, remarrying, starting a second family, caregiving for either children or parents, taking a sabbatical, retiring, beginning a second career, and grandparenting. Fundraisers need to be in touch with their donors through surveys, research, visits, and phone calls in order to recognize when to solicit major gifts and when to make more modest requests.

Recognize That Fundraising Among the Affluent Has Two Valuable Pluses

When you fundraise among affluent households, there are two valuable extra results:

1. *More of the fundraising income will be less restricted.* The higher the gift amount, the more likely that the donor will have a specific project or program in mind for it. It is easier to encourage donors who give in the mid-range to designate rather than restrict their gifts or to leave gift use fully to the judgment of the organization.

2. *You will be less dependent on the whims of one or two donors.* All fundraisers have been there: for two or three years, Mr. and Mrs. Jones have given the top gift to your not-for-profit. You've become accustomed to counting on their continuing generosity. Suddenly, for whatever reason, this year's gift doesn't come, and you're scrambling to make up 30, 40, or 50 percent of your gift income.

Focus on Renewal and Upgrading Rather Than Acquisition

If you lose a donor, you must find a new one. As it is five times more difficult to acquire new donors than to renew existing ones, it makes sense to focus on keeping and increasing the support from those who already give. And because Americans are living longer, the value of a renewing donor is increasing dramatically. This is the rationale underlying an *after-marketing* approach that makes renewal and upgrading rather than acquisition the priority of the development strategy. The case study report in Chapter Eight recommends renewal of existing donors as a major development strategy for a specific organization.

Focusing on after marketing helps increase the retention of baby boomers and other individuals born after World War II. Midlife and younger persons are more likely than mature Americans to be *shoppers* in every aspect of their lives, including philanthropy. They show less loyalty than do mature civics.

Your goal is to help the donors choose your organization as their charitable priority. This requires a carefully selected series of informational and appeal steps. As soon as a gift is made, the cycle of renewed gift giving must begin. Recognition and appreciation needs to be given on a regular basis. Creating *core* donors means shortening the time between the first and second gifts and then moving donors up the loyalty ladder.

Many of the more successful not-for-profits have shortened their renewal periods to thirty, forty-five, or sixty days. They use a combination of formal acknowledgment, appreciation, and recognition steps (an *after-marketing matrix*) that maximizes donors' number of contacts with the organization in the days immediately after a gift is received. A formal after-marketing matrix encourages strong bonding during the earliest phases of the donor's relationship with the not-for-profit. An after-marketing strategy should be put in place to maximize donor retention and encourage multiple gifts and upgrading.

To summarize, prior to starting your development assessment, identify your underlying fundraising strategic assumptions and summarize them in a short document. (The sample report in Chapter Eight illustrates this step.) This document is the rationale for your recommendations and will guide your conclusions.

Part Three

Gathering the Information You Need

Where to Look: Resources for Environmental Scanning

USING THE DEVELOPMENT ASSESSMENT PROCESS, you compile your information from many sources, internal and external, before making recommendations. Here are some of the internal and external information sources you can use.

Beginning with Your Internal Resources

The organization's own case statement, mission, and strategic documents should always be reviewed early on in the process. Get copies of all the available written materials and read through them before beginning interviews.

A caution: because not-for-profits often do not undertake long-range planning on a regular basis, these documents are often out of date or in need of revision. If so, the assessment will need to point that out. Do not attempt to do the long-range planning as part of the assessment. A development assessment complements institutional planning but does not take the place of the organization's own documents detailing its master plan, strategic plans, and goals and objectives.

Also, use your meetings with staff effectively. Although meetings with the top leadership staff are expected, also seek out those who have been with the organization the longest. They can provide you with an oral history often otherwise unavailable.

Scanning Nationally and Beyond

Although *Transforming Fundraising* provides a good overview of national demographic and philanthropic trends, you should do some primary research of your own. The following resources can help you.

National Charitable Statistics

American Association of Fund-Raising Counsel. *Giving USA.* (Published annually.)

National Center for Charitable Statistics. (http://nccs.urban.org/states.htm)

National Society of Fund Raising Executives. (800–666-FUND or http://www.nsfre.org)

Database and Internet Resources

Virtually anyone with a personal computer and modem can gain access to hundreds of information sources, ranging from directories and bibliographic indexes to full-text sources from which you can print out an entire article. Here are a few of the more popular services that offer subscription databases or information on disk:

CDA InvestNet. (Ft. Lauderdale, Fla.; 800–345–7334)

Data Times. (Oklahoma City, Okla.; 800–751–6400)

DIALOG Information Services. (Palo Alto, Calif.; 800–334–2564)

Dow Jones News/Retrieval. (800–522–3567, ext. 52)

Dun & Bradstreet. *Asian/Pacific Disc.* (800–526–0651)

Dun & Bradstreet. *Dun's Business Locator.* (800–526–0651)

Dun & Bradstreet. *Dun's Million Dollar Disc.* (800–526–0651)

Dun & Bradstreet Information Services. (800–872–4349)

Reed Reference. *Complete Marquis Who's Who Plus.* (800–521–8100)

Reed Reference. *Corporate Affiliations Plus.* (800–521–8100)

Reed Reference. *Martindale-Hubbell Law Directory.* (800–521–8100)

Books and Reports on Demographic Trends

I consistently use these books and reports on demographics and trends:

Barna, George. *The Barna Report: 1992–1993.*

Blank, Renee, and Sandra Slipp. *Voices of Diversity.*

Bond, Jonathan, and Richard Kirshenbaum. *Under the Radar: Talking to Today's Cynical Consumer.*

Burnett, Ken. *Relationship Fund Raising.*

Dunn, William. *Selling the Story: The Layman's Guide to Collecting and Communicating Demographic Information.*

Dychtwald, Ken, with Joe Flower. *Agewave.*

Fiancee, Peter, and Rebecca Piirto. *Capturing Customers: How to Target the Hottest Markets of the '90s.*

Foot, David K. *Boom, Bust and Echo: How to Profit from the Coming Demographic Shift.*

Guber, Selina S., and Jon Berry. *Marketing to and Through Kids.*

Jones, Landon Y. *Great Expectations: America and the Baby Boom Generation.*

Leeming, E. Janice, and Cynthia F. Tripp. *Segmenting the Women's Market: Using Niche Marketing to Understand and Meet the Diverse Needs of Today's Most Dynamic Consumer Market.*

Miller, Eric, and the Editors of *Research Alert. The Lifestyle Odyssey: The Facts Behind the Social, Personal, and Cultural Changes Touching Each of Our Lives.*

Morgan, Carol M., and Doran J. Levy. *Segmenting the Mature Market: Identifying, Targeting and Reaching America's Diverse, Booming Senior Markets.*

Morrison, Ian, and Greg Schmidt. *Future Tense: The Business Realities of the Next Ten Years.*

Myers, Gerry. *Targeting the New Professional Woman.*

Ostroff, Jeff. *Successful Marketing to the 50+ Consumer.*

Piirto, Rebecca. *Beyond Mind Games: The Marketing Power of Psychographics.*

Roberts, Sam. *Who We Are: A Portrait of America.*

Rossman, Marlene L. *Multicultural Marketing.*

Russell, Cheryl. *The Master Trend: How the Baby Boom Generation Is Remaking America.*

Shaw, Sondra C., and Martha A. Taylor. *Reinventing Fundraising: Realizing the Potential of Women's Philanthropy.*

Sherden, William A. *Market Ownership: The Art and Science of Becoming #1.*

Stanley, Thomas J. *Marketing to the Affluent, Selling to the Affluent, Networking with the Affluent.*

Strauss, William, and Neil Howe. *Generations: The History of America's Future, 1584 to 2069.*

Thau, Richard D., and Jay S. Heflin (eds.). *Generations Apart: Xers vs. Boomers vs. the Elderly.*

Thompson, Anne I., and Andrea R. Kaminski. *Women and Philanthropy.*

Tingley, Judith C. *Genderflex: Men and Women Speaking Each Other's Language at Work.*

von Schlegell, Abbie J., and Joan M. Fisher (eds.). *Women as Donors, Women as Philanthropists* (New Directions for Philanthropic Fundraising, no. 2).

Waldrop, Judith, with Marcia Mogelonsky. *The Seasons of Business: The Marketer's Guide to Consumer Behavior.*

Weinstein, Art. *Market Segmentation: Using Demographics, Psychographics and Other Niche Marketing Techniques to Predict Customer Behavior.*

Wolfe, David B. *Marketing to Boomers and Beyond.*

Scanning Regionally and Locally

Once you've scanned the national demographic and philanthropic trends, you should also review carefully what is happening in your regional and local community, both demographically and philanthropically. *Be careful!* Your particular geographical area may neatly fit the national demographic and philanthropic patterns discussed but don't take this for granted.

You will need to scan the regional and local environment to learn what is happening demographically. Your questions (as the sample survey in Chapter Seven shows) will include these: What is the population makeup by sex, racial or ethnic background, age, education, and so forth? Is this makeup stable or changing? How is the population doing economically? Are there pockets of affluence? Is the region prospering?

You will also need to review the local philanthropic trends: What is happening philanthropically? Has giving by individuals, by foundations, and by corporations increased or decreased? Are there more or fewer not-for-profits? Are there any major capital campaigns in the offing? If so, what are the campaign goals? Are any campaigns about to finish? Were they fully successful in meeting their goals? If not, why?

Much of the information your organization needs about regional and local area demographics will have to be gathered from external resources. As the assessment coordinator, you must find the most current resources. The best sources for local comparisons include local United Way agencies, local community foundations, and the colleagues with whom you network at professional meetings, such as meetings of your local chapter of the National Society of Fund Raising Executives (NSFRE). You may use any or all of the following sources:

U.S. Department of Commerce Census Reports

U.S. Bureau of the Census. *County and City Data Book: A Statistical Abstract Supplement.* (Summaries of census data; much useful information; issued periodically.)

U.S. Bureau of the Census. *Hidden Treasures, Census Bureau Data and Where to Find It!* (Services and telephone numbers.)

State Resources

Independent Sector. *Nonprofit Almanac 1996–1997: Dimensions of the Independent Sector.* (Independent Sector, 1828 "L" Street NW, Washington, DC 20036; 202–223–8100)

The State Nonprofit Almanac 1997. (Profiles of charitable organizations.) (United Press of America, 4720 Boston Way, Lanham, MD 20706; 800–462–6420)

Local Officials, Organizations, and Government

Local officials from both the public and private sectors are often a good source of information about large issues facing any given community, but beware of special interests and self-serving presentations of selected information.

Local governments, particularly county governments, are often excellent sources of information on demographic and economic data projections, future housing sites, and transportation planning.

Hospital departments of community social services and human service agencies that serve particular target populations often track data on the extent and impact of homelessness, drug problems, dysfunctional families, and needs in child care and elder care, literacy, health, and transportation.

School districts maintain a close watch on demographics as they do their planning.

United Ways often develop community needs assessments to determine criteria for funding. United Way priorities and future funding projections are also significant planning information.

Local foundations often have good information on community needs and problems.

Local chambers of commerce often have very useful data on business and industry growth in their areas.

Colleges and universities often conduct research and studies that result in useful social and economic information. Check whether your local college or university has a marketing department or a school of urban studies.

In addition, *local organizations, banks, and businesses* often have very useful information that is indicative of demographic trends and economic patterns.

Fundraising Resources

There's no reason to reinvent the fundraising wheel. As you go through the process of deciding which strategies make the most sense for your organization, let the research of your professional colleagues guide you.

Here is a list of some of the best thinking in the field, gathered and expanded from Bookworks, a list compiled by the National Society of Fund Raising Executives. (The latest version of this list can be accessed on the Internet at http://www.nsfre.org.)

Fundraising: General

Broce, Thomas E. *Fund Raising: The Guide to Raising Money from Private Sources.*

Burnett, Ken. *Relationship Fundraising.*

Cumerford, William R. *Start-to-Finish Fund Raising: How a Professional Organizes and Conducts a Successful Campaign.*

Flanagan, Joan. *The Grass Roots Fundraising Book: How to Raise Money in Your Community.*

Flanagan, Joan. *Successful Fundraising: A Complete Handbook for Volunteers and Professionals.*

Graham, Christine. *Keep the Money Coming: A Step-by-Step Strategic Guide to Annual Fundraising.*

Greenfield, James M. *Fund-Raising Fundamentals: A Guide to Annual Giving for Professionals and Volunteers.*

Krit, Robert L. *The Fund Raising Handbook.*

Poderis, Tony. *It's a Great Day to Fund-Raise! A Veteran Campaigner Reveals the Development Tips and Techniques That Will Work for You.*

Rosso, Henry A., and Associates. *Achieving Excellence in Fundraising: A Comprehensive Guide to Principles, Strategies, and Methods.*

Seymour, Harold J. *Designs for Fund Raising: Principles, Patterns, Techniques.*

Warner, Irving R. *The Art of Fund Raising: The Classic Primer.*

Not-for-Profit Planning, Marketing, and Management

Amherst H. Wilder Foundation. *Collaboration: What Makes It Work.*

Amherst H. Wilder Foundation. *Marketing Workbook for Nonprofit Organizations.*

Andreasen, Alan R. *Marketing Social Change: Changing Behavior to Promote Health, Social Development, and the Environment.*

Barry, B. W. *Strategic Planning Workbook for Nonprofit Organizations* (Amherst H. Wilder Foundation).

Berendt, Robert, and J. Richard Taft. *How to Rate Your Development Office.*

Bryce, Herrington. *Financial and Strategic Management for Nonprofit Organizations.*

Bryson, John M. *Strategic Planning for Public and Nonprofit Organizations: A Guide to Strengthening and Sustaining Organizational Achievement.*

Conners, Tracy Daniel. *The Nonprofit Management Handbook.*

Gingold, Diane. *Strategic Philanthropy in the 1990's. Handbook of Corporate Development Strategies for Nonprofit Managers.*

Greenfield, James M. *Fund Raising: Evaluating and Managing the Fund Development Process.*

Grønbjerg, Kirsten A. *Understanding Nonprofit Funding: Managing Revenues in Social Services and Community Development Organizations.*

Herman, Robert D., and Associates. *The Jossey-Bass Handbook of Nonprofit Leadership and Management.*

Kets de Vries, Manfred F. R. *Life and Death in the Executive Fast Lane: Essays on Irrational Organizations and Their Leaders.*

Kotler, Philip. *Marketing for Nonprofit Organizations.*

Kotler, Philip, and Alan R. Andreasen. *Strategic Marketing for Nonprofit Organizations.*

Kouzes, James M., and Barry Z. Posner. *The Leadership Challenge: How to Keep Getting Extraordinary Things Done in Organizations.*

Lindahl, Wesley E. *Strategic Planning for Fund Raising.*

Lord, James Gregory. *Philanthropy and Marketing.*

Lynch, Richard. *LEAD! How Public and Nonprofit Managers Can Bring Out the Best in Themselves and Their Organizations.*

Nichols, Judith E. *Growing from Good to Great: Positioning Your Fundraising Efforts for Big Gains.*

Nichols, Judith E. *Targeted Fund Raising: Defining and Refining Your Development Strategy.*

Nonprofit Organizations' Business Forms (disk edition).

Peter F. Drucker Foundation for Nonprofit Management. *The Drucker Foundation Self-Assessment Tool for Nonprofit Organizations.*

Smith, Bucklin, & Associates. *The Complete Guide to Nonprofit Management.*

Not-for-Profit Boards

Carver, John. *Boards That Make a Difference: A New Design for Leadership in Nonprofit and Public Organizations.*

Carver, John. *Empowering Boards for Leadership: Redefining Excellence in Governance.*

Houle, Cyril O. *Governing Boards.*

Howe, Fisher. *The Board Member's Guide to Fund Raising.*

Howe, Fisher. *Welcome to the Board: Your Guide to Effective Participation for All Nonprofit Trustees.*

O'Connell, Brian. *The Board Member's Book: Making a Difference in Voluntary Organizations.*

Panas, Jerold. *Boardroom Verities: A Celebration of Trusteeship with Some Guides and Techniques to Govern By.*

Seiler, Timothy L., and Kay Sprinkel Grace (eds.). *Achieving Trustee Involvement in Fundraising* (New Directions for Philanthropic Fundraising, no. 4).

Zander, Alvin. *Making Boards Effective: The Dynamics of Nonprofit Governing Boards.*

Major Gifts

Donovan, James A. *Take the Fear Out of Asking for Major Gifts.*

Dove, Kent E. *Conducting a Successful Capital Campaign.*

Panas, Jerold. *Mega Gifts: Who Gives Them, Who Gets Them.*

Prince, Russ Alan, and Karen Maru File. *The Seven Faces of Philanthropy: A New Approach to Cultivating Major Donors.*

Planned Giving

Ashton, Debra. *The Complete Guide to Planned Giving.*

Jordan, R. R., and K. L. Quynn. *Planned Giving: Management, Marketing, and Law.*

Schmeling, David G. *Planned Giving for the One Person Development Office.*

Sharpe, Robert F. *The Planned Giving Idea Book.*

Proposals and Grants

Carlson, Mim. *Winning Grants Step by Step: Support Centers of America's Complete Workbook for Planning, Developing, and Writing Successful Proposals.*

Geever, J. C. *The Foundation Center's Guide to Proposal Writing.*

Huntsinger, Jerald E. *Fund Raising Letters.*

Murray, Vic. *Improving Corporate Donations: New Strategies for Grantmakers and Grantseekers.*

Shannon, James P. (ed.). *The Corporate Contributions Handbook: Devoting Private Means to Public Needs.*

Direct Mail

Lautman, Kay, and Henry Goldstein. *Dear Friend.*

Smith, George. *Asking Properly.*

Warwick, Mal. *How to Write Successful Fundraising Letters.*

Warwick, Mal. *999 Tips, Trends, and Guidelines for Direct Mail and Telephone Fund Raising.*

Warwick, Mal. *Raising Money by Mail.*

Warwick, Mal. *Revolution in the Mailbox.*

Warwick, Mal. *Technology and the Future of Fundraising.*

Warwick, Mal. *You Don't Always Get What You Ask For.*

Special Events

Devney, Darcy Campion. *Organizing Special Events and Conferences.*

Gatherwood, D. W. *The Complete Guide to Special Event Management: Business Insights, Financial Advice, and Successful Strategies from Ernst & Young.*

Goldblatt, Joe Jeff. *Special Events: The Art and Science of Celebration.*

Plessner, Gerald M. *The Encyclopedia of Fund Raising.* Vol. 1: *Charity Auction Management Manual.*

Plessner, Gerald M. *The Encyclopedia of Fund Raising.* Vol. 2: *Golf Tournament Management Manual.*

Plessner, Gerald M. *The Encyclopedia of Fund Raising.* Vol. 3: *Testimonial Dinner and Industry Luncheon Management Manual.*

Whitcomb, Nike B. *Money Makers: A Systematic Approach to Special Event Fund Raising.*

Prospect Research and Demographics

Bowen, William G., Thomas I. Nygren, Sarah E. Turner, and Elizabeth A. Duffy. *The Charitable Nonprofits: An Analysis of Institutional Dynamics and Characteristics.*

Joseph, James A. *Remaking America: How the Benevolent Traditions of Many Cultures Are Transforming Our National Life.*

McCarthy, Kathleen D. *Women's Culture: American Philanthropy and Art 1830–1930.*

Nichols, Judith E. *Changing Demographics: Fund Raising in the 1990's: Using Demographics and Psychographics to Improve Your Fund Raising Efforts.*

Nichols, Judith E. *Global Demographics.*

Nichols, Judith E. *Pinpointing Affluence: Increasing Your Share of Major Donor Dollars.*

Norsworthy, A. (ed.). *FRI [Fund Raising Institute] Prospect Research Resource Directory.*

Shaw, Sondra C., and Martha A. Taylor. *Reinventing Fundraising: Realizing the Potential of Women's Philanthropy.*

von Schlegell, Abbie J., and Joan M. Fisher (eds.). *Women as Donors, Women as Philanthropists* (New Directions for Philanthropic Fundraising, no. 2).

Philanthropy

Bremner, Robert H. *American Philanthropy.*

Bremner, Robert H. *Giving: Charity and Philanthropy in History.*

Burlingame, Dwight F. (ed.). *The Responsibilities of Wealth.*

Lawson, Douglas M. *Give to Live: How Giving Can Change Your Life.*

Lohmann, Roger A. *The Commons: New Perspectives on Nonprofit Organizations and Voluntary Organizations.*

Martin, Mike W. *Virtuous Giving.*

Mixer, Joseph R. *Principles of Professional Fundraising: Useful Foundations for Successful Practice.*

O'Connell, Brian (ed.). *America's Voluntary Spirit: A Book of Readings.*

O'Connell, Brian. *Philanthropy in Action.*

O'Neill, Michael. *The Third America: The Emergence of the Nonprofit Sector in the United States.*

Payton, Robert L. *Philanthropy: Voluntary Action for the Public Good.*

Rosenberg, Claude N., Jr. *Wealthy and Wise: How You and America Can Get the Most out of Your Giving.*

Schwartz, John. J. *Modern American Philanthropy: A Personal Account.*

Seltzer, Michael (ed.). *Fundraising Matters: True Stories of How Raising Funds Fulfills Dreams* (New Directions for Philanthropic Fundraising, no. 1).

Fundraising: A Profession

Burlingame, Dwight F., and Lamont J. Hulse. *Taking Fund Raising Seriously: Advancing the Profession and Practice of Raising Money.*

Gurin, Maurice G. *Confessions of a Fund Raiser: Lessons of an Instructive Career.*

Knauft, E. B., Renee A. Berger, and Sandra T. Gray. *Profiles of Excellence: Achieving Success in the Nonprofit Sector.*

Knott, Ronald Alan. *The Makings of a Philanthropic Fundraiser: The Instructive Example of Milton Murray.*

National Society of Fund Raising Executives. *The NSFRE Profile: 1995 Membership Survey.*

Panas, Jerold. *Born to Raise: What Makes a Great Fundraiser, What Makes a Fundraiser Great.*

Powell, James Lawrence. *Pathways to Leadership: How to Achieve and Sustain Success.*

Not-for-Profit Law, Tax, and Accounting

Bachman, Steve. *Nonprofit Litigation: A Practical Guide with Forms and Checklists.*

Blazek, Jody. *Tax Planning and Compliance for Tax-Exempt Organizations: Forms, Checklists, Procedures.*

Greenfield, James M. (ed.). *Financial Practices for Effective Fundraising* (New Directions for Philanthropic Fundraising, no. 3).

Gross, Malvern J., Jr., Richard F. Larkin, Roger S. Bruttomesso, and John J. McNally. *Financial and Accounting Guide for Not-for-Profit Organizations* (5th edition).

Hopkins, Bruce R. *Charity, Advocacy, and the Law.*

Hopkins, Bruce R. *The Law of Fund Raising.*

Hopkins, Bruce R. *The Law of Tax-Exempt Organizations.*

Hopkins, Bruce R. *A Legal Guide to Starting and Managing a Nonprofit Organization.*

Hopkins, Bruce R. *Nonprofit Law Dictionary.*

Hopkins, Bruce R. *The Tax Law of Charitable Giving.*

Sanders, Michael I. *Partnerships and Joint Ventures Involving Tax-Exempt Organizations.*

Ethics

Briscoe, Dianne G. (ed.). *Ethics in Fundraising: Putting Values into Practice.* (New Directions for Philanthropic Fundraising, no. 6).

Pastin, Mark. *The Hard Problems of Management: Gaining the Ethics Edge.*

General Interest

American Association of Fund-Raising Counsel. *Giving USA.* (Published annually.)

National Society of Fund Raising Executives. *Glossary of Fund Raising Terms.*

Panas, Jerold. *Official Fundraising Almanac: Facts, Figures, and Anecdotes from and for Fundraisers.*

Philanthropic Service for Institutions. *Accent on Humor: The Wit and Wisdom of Wealth and Philanthropy.*

Chapter 7

Sample Forms for Surveying, Data Collection, and Information Recording

THIS CHAPTER contains sample documents you can use in gathering and organizing the materials and information you need to collect.

The Assessment Folder

To keep things in order, it's best to create an assessment folder divided into the assessment's major sections, including mission and vision, financial, leadership, fundraising, and public relations. Each section should have a file section of its own, and all material should be coded and filed in the relevant section. Sometimes a document will pertain to more than one section. You can either file it in both places or cross-reference it.

Two Record-Keeping Forms and the Survey

Checklist for Data Collection

As information is gathered, the assessment coordinator should keep a checklist, like the one shown in the Sample Checklist for Data Collection, in order to have an overview of what is in the assessment folder and what is missing. It will probably be necessary to gather the materials on the checklist from a number of individuals. Be sure to keep track of who has agreed to be responsible for providing specific pieces of information. Knowing where both the resistance to change and the willingness to cooperate are located in an organization will be important in planning fundraising strategy.

SAMPLE CHECKLIST FOR DATA COLLECTION

Materials Requested   **Received (Date and Person)**

I. GENERAL BACKGROUND

    A. Demographic background   _____

    B. Climate for fundraising   _____

II. ORGANIZATIONAL BACKGROUND

    A. General   _____

    B. Mission and vision   _____

    C. Financial   _____

    D. Leadership   _____

        1. Board of trustees   _____

        2. Executive director or CEO   _____

        3. Program director(s)   _____

III. FUNDRAISING

    A. Fundraising history   _____

    B. Budget   _____

    C. Donor profile   _____

    D. Prospect pool profile   _____

    E. Donor demographic profile   _____

    F. Overall fundraising strategy   _____

    G. Computerization   _____

    H. Stewardship and accountability   _____

    I. Gift acknowledgment and recognition   _____

    J. Fundraising methodologies   _____

        1. Major (individual) gifts   _____

        2. Planned giving   _____

        3. Annual fundraising   _____

        4. Corporate and foundation giving   _____

SAMPLE CHECKLIST FOR DATA COLLECTION (continued)

Materials Requested   **Received (Date and Person)**

    5.   Special events   _____

    6.   Other fundraising income   _____

  K. Fundraising staffing

    1.   Job descriptions   _____

    2.   Organizational chart   _____

    3.   Director of development   _____

    4.   Other professional staff   _____

    5.   Support staff   _____

  L. Fundraising resources

    1.   Professional growth opportunities   _____

    2.   Resource library   _____

    3.   Idea generation   _____

IV. PUBLIC RELATIONS, IMAGE, OUTREACH

  A. The view from outside   _____

  B. Media resources   _____

V. ADDITIONAL INFORMATION

_____

_____

_____

_____

_____

_____

_____

_____

_____

Form for Information Recording

Use another form like the Sample Form for Recording Survey Information to record the highlights of the information received from the survey so you can ensure that the main points of the assessment have been covered and to create an outline summary that the report narrative can be built on (use extra sheets of paper, of course!).

The Assessment Survey

The assessment survey form shown in the following pages is a sample. You may need to adjust it to better serve your particular organization. If your not-for-profit offers memberships as well as solicits donations, for example, you will want to include sections on both donors and members. Try, however, to follow the sample survey's main categories.

As described in Chapters One and Two, the assessment survey is the assessment coordinator's main vehicle for collecting historical data on an organization. The completed survey provides the framework for a step-by-step analysis of the components that either directly or indirectly affect the success of an organization's development program.

Typically, the assessment coordinator in cooperation with the executive director decides who can best handle each of the various survey sections. Each section is then given to the responsible individual, with a covering memo summarizing the rationale for the assessment and spelling out the specifics of what is being asked: that is, to provide the information requested in survey section X and to forward it to the assessment coordinator on or before a specific date. Again, use as many sheets of paper as necessary to answer all questions fully.

During interviews and meetings and in soliciting responses to the assessment survey questions and forms, encourage participants to give more rather than less information. Series of questions are included to encourage respondents to think beyond specifics on the data collection queries.

Collect documentation in whatever form it can be provided. Often the return of a form or answers to a series of questions from the survey will suggest a need for in-person follow-up. A department or program head, for example, might need help in articulating his or her full scope of fundraising needs—especially if he or she has learned over the years to ask for less rather than more. A particular comment on a form might open a new path of speculation for you. Or the inability to answer a survey question may help respondents recognize a need to start gathering information in that area.

SAMPLE FORM FOR RECORDING SURVEY INFORMATION

Area	Strengths	Concerns	Recommendations
I. GENERAL BACKGROUND			
A. Demographic background			
B. Climate for fundraising			
II. ORGANIZATIONAL BACKGROUND			
A. General			
B. Mission and vision			
C. Financial			
D. Leadership			
1. Board of trustees			
2. Executive director or CEO			
3. Program director(s)			

SAMPLE FORM FOR RECORDING SURVEY INFORMATION (continued)

Area	Strengths	Concerns	Recommendations
III. FUNDRAISING			
A. Fundraising history			
B. Budget			
C. Donor profile			
D. Prospect pool profile			
E. Donor demographic profile			
F. Overall fundraising strategy			
G. Computerization			
H. Stewardship and accountability			
I. Gift acknowledgment and recognition			

J.   Fundraising methodologies

1.   Major (individual) gifts

2.   Planned giving

3.   Annual fundraising

4.   Corporate and foundation giving

5.   Special events

6.   Other fundraising income

K.   Fundraising staffing

1.   Job descriptions

2.   Organizational chart

3.   Director of development

4.   Other professional development staff

5.   Support staff

SAMPLE FORM FOR RECORDING SURVEY INFORMATION (continued)

Area	Strengths	Concerns	Recommendations
L. Fundraising resources			
1. Professional growth opportunities			
2. Resource library			
3. Idea generation			
IV. PUBLIC RELATIONS, IMAGE, OUTREACH			
A. The view from outside			
B. Media resources			
V. ADDITIONAL INFORMATION			

SAMPLE ASSESSMENT SURVEY

I. GENERAL BACKGROUND

A. Demographic background

Use any available resources: Census Bureau, chamber of commerce, United Way.

Key Questions to Answer

- What significant demographic and economic trends does your organization need to be aware of?

- What impact are these demographic and economic trends likely to have on donors' ability to give more?

- Define area demographics.

  What is your organization's area of service geographically (local, regional, national, or international)?

  What is the current population makeup? By gender? By age? By racial or ethnic background? By education? By other measures (describe them)?

  How is the population in the area doing economically? Are there pockets of affluence? Is the region prospering or depressed?

  What is the expected population growth in your organization's area for the next five to ten years?

  Is population makeup in the area changing? Is it changing by gender? By racial or ethnic background? By age? By education? By other measures (describe them)?

B. Climate for fundraising

Key Questions to Answer

- What external factors could affect your organization's ability to raise money?

- How sophisticated is your organization's fundraising?

- How strongly positioned has your organization been vis-à-vis other organizations with similar missions?

- How does United Way see the funding trends?

- What are the regulations that affect your organization's fundraising? Are any changes coming?

- Define your organization's geographical area of possible supporters.

- How philanthropic is the population? How philanthropic are individuals? Corporations? Foundations?

- Have there been any recent changes in the funding climate, or are you anticipating changes (such as corporate mergers, the death of a key philanthropist, or the availability of new foundations)?

- Is your organization's funding being affected by government cuts? What specific dollars and programs have been cut? What are the implications?

- Is your organization's funding being affected by United Way allocations? What specific dollars and programs have been cut or increased? What are the implications?

- How many not-for-profits are in your organization's area?

  Are any major fundraising campaigns under way? If they are, by whom? How much are these campaigns trying to raise?

  How sophisticated is other not-for-profits' fundraising generally?

  Are any of these other organizations providing similar programs and services? If they are, provide the names of these organizations.

  How well is your organization positioned in terms of dollars raised? In terms of recognition?

- Could a collaborative program be launched by your organization and a "competitor"? Describe what this program might look like.

- What partnerships could your organization forge in the community in order to better deliver its services and carry out its mission? Describe them.

II. ORGANIZATIONAL BACKGROUND

A. General

- When does your organization's fiscal year begin and end?

- Describe your organization's history, including the answers to these questions: When was the organization founded? Why? By whom? Provide any documentation available.

- Describe how your organization is structured. Provide the organizational chart. Explain any significant recent changes.

B. Mission and vision

Key Questions to Answer

- Do your organization's fundraising goals have a basis in the needs of the community and the organization?

- What is your organization's fundraising goal for this year? For next year? For the next three to five years?

  How do these goals relate to needs?

  Have additional resources been committed? Staff? Equipment? Materials?

- What is your organization's vision? What is its mission? Provide any strategic plans or documents that give insight about the vision and mission.

- What is the *case* your organization will make to donors and prospects? How is your organization *unique?*

- How does your organization determine organizational goals? How does it get board input? Staff input? Volunteer input? Community input?

- What are the specific programs your organization wants funded for this year? For next year? For three to five years out? For five to ten years out?

  How have the programs been determined?

  How much will the programs cost? How have the costs been determined? Has inflation been factored in?

  What are the program priorities?

- What words best describe your organization? Does it have a clear *personality?* Use the following list.[1] (Check all that apply.)

____ Passionate	____ Rigid	____ Compassionate	____ Large
____ Visionary	____ Bold	____ Outspoken	____ Dynamic
____ Tired	____ Focused	____ Inspiring	____ Leadership
____ Bureaucratic	____ Justice	____ Catalytic	____ Determined
____ Changing	____ Exciting	____ Cautious	____ Conservative
____ Fun	____ Rich	____ Established	____ Entrepreneurial
____ Staid	____ Persistent	____ Complacent	____ Other (be specific)

- When was the last time your organization reviewed its vision and mission?

- What are your organization's strengths? What makes it unique?

- What are your organization's vulnerabilities?

---

1. Adapted with permission from Joe Saxton, 17th International Fund Raising Workshop, Amsterdam, 1997.

C. Financial

- Translate your organization's goals or objectives into financial needs, indicating the dollars needed both by type of need and by immediacy. First, record this information on the Financial Needs form provided here (or create a similar form), using the following definitions of types of need. Second, describe what is covered by each program or service to be funded. (You may need to ask each program director to fill out a Financial Needs form and provide a description.)

  Operating needs: unrestricted funding for programs and services that are offered on an ongoing basis. Includes staffing and operational costs (rent, materials, and so forth). Best served by gifts from donors who are willing to let the organization determine the *area of greatest need. Target audiences:* those who may give repeating (annual) gifts of smaller amounts.

  Capital needs: restricted funding for specific projects or programs that arise as special needs. Includes facility building and renovation, equipment purchase and upgrading, and so forth. *Target audiences:* those who may give one-time gifts of, typically, $1,000 and more.

  Endowment needs: unrestricted and restricted funding that creates a *safety net* for the organization. Typically recommended as the capital needed to produce 20 percent of the operating needs. *Target audiences:* those who may give bequest and life income gifts.

SAMPLE FORM: FINANCIAL NEEDS

Type or Program	Operating Needs	Capital Needs	Endowment Needs
IMMEDIATE NEEDS			
_____(program)	$_____	$_____	$_____
_____(program)	$_____	$_____	$_____
_____(program)	$_____	$_____	$_____
Total $$ needed	$_____	$_____	$_____
NEEDS IN 3–5 YEARS			
_____(program)	$_____	$_____	$_____
_____(program)	$_____	$_____	$_____
_____(program)	$_____	$_____	$_____
Total $$ needed	$_____	$_____	$_____
NEEDS IN 5–10 YEARS			
_____(program)	$_____	$_____	$_____
_____(program)	$_____	$_____	$_____
_____(program)	$_____	$_____	$_____
Total $$ needed	$_____	$_____	$_____

- Define the overall financial stability of your organization:

  ___*Stable*: reserves in place; operating comfortably in the black.

  ___*Pre-edge*: overextended, but problems are manageable.

  ___*At the edge*: beginning to feel a sense of crisis; cash flow problematic.

  ___*Over the edge*: in crisis, potential for immediate closure.

D. Leadership

   1. Board of trustees

Key Questions to Answer

- Do the board and the community understand your organization's mission, goals, and objectives?

- Do they view your organization as a leader?

- Is the board representative of the community?

- Provide bylaws; provide board and committee structure chart with assignments; provide board job description.

- How is recruitment to the board handled?

  How are potential board members identified?

  How are potential board members cultivated?

  What is the nominating process?

  How are committee assignments determined?

- How is orientation accomplished?

  Is there a new member meeting or retreat?

  Is there a folder or notebook? Provide a copy.

- Is the population of the community represented on the board? Provide a list of board members, with officers and terms shown. Provide biographies or résumés; include a short assessment of *giving and getting* potential.

  How many women and members of minorities serve on the board?

  Is the population your organization serves represented?

  Indicate on the board list, next to each name, the board members' giving histories.

Use the following outline to determine overall board giving and getting.

Board Giving

- How does the board give? Do its members make leadership gifts? Annual gifts? Do they attend special events?

- What is the average size of board personal gifts? What is the highest gift? The lowest gift?

- What percentage of the board gives?

- Is the board making meaningful gifts (giving at or near its capacity)?

Board Getting

- Does the board ask for money? Do its members ask for leadership gifts? Annual gifts? Attendance at special events? Corporate gifts?

- How well does it ask for money?

- How actively does it ask for money?

- What percentage of members participate?

- Does the board receive fundraising training? If it does, how does it receive this training?

2. Executive director or CEO

(This section is to be completed by the executive director or CEO.)

- Provide a current vita or résumé and a job description.

- How much of your time is spent in networking activities?

- How much of your time is spent with other not-for-profits?

- How much of your time is spent in active fundraising?

- Describe your skills in the following areas:

  Public speaking

  People skills

  Fundraising

  Cultivation and solicitation

- Where—if anywhere—do you feel you need further training?

- Are there any management problems, such as low staff morale?

3. Program director(s)

(This section is to be completed by each program director.)

- Provide a current vita or résumé.

- How much of your time is spent in networking activities?

- How much of your time is spent with other not-for-profits?
- How much of your time is spent in active fundraising?
- Describe your skills in the following areas:

  Public speaking

  People skills

  Fundraising

  Cultivation and solicitation
- Where—if anywhere—do you feel you need further training?

III. FUNDRAISING

Key Questions to Answer

- Are your organization's fundraising goals realistic?

  Where can donations come from and in what amounts?

  What amount comes from individuals? Foundations? Corporations? Special events? Bequests?

- What fundraising measurements does your organization use?

  What are the dollars spent compared to the dollars raised?

  What is the increase of return on the dollar over the last time period?

  What is the increase in the donor base?

  What is the increase in the prospect base?

- How well does your organization plan its fundraising?

  Are budget constraints managed?

  Do action steps occur at planned intervals?

  What is the number of proposals submitted? What percentage of proposals submitted are funded?

  Is face-to-face contact maintained with donors, prospects, and board members?

  When is planning done?

A. Fundraising history

- Provide fundraising budgets for the last three fiscal years or complete the Fundraising History form provided here, writing in the years at the column heads.

SAMPLE FORM: FUNDRAISING HISTORY

	Fundraising Income for Last Three Years			Fundraising Expenses for Last Three Years		
	Year ___	Year ___	Year ___	Year ___	Year ___	Year ___
TOTAL $$ RAISED OR SPENT	$_____	$_____	$_____	$_____	$_____	$_____
BY CATEGORY						
Annual giving	$_____	$_____	$_____	$_____	$_____	$_____
Direct mail	$_____	$_____	$_____	$_____	$_____	$_____
Phone-a-thon	$_____	$_____	$_____	$_____	$_____	$_____
Face-to-face	$_____	$_____	$_____	$_____	$_____	$_____
Major giving	$_____	$_____	$_____	$_____	$_____	$_____
Planned giving	$_____	$_____	$_____	$_____	$_____	$_____
Realized bequests	$_____	$_____	$_____	$_____	$_____	$_____
New expectancies	$_____	$_____	$_____	$_____	$_____	$_____
Corporate	$_____	$_____	$_____	$_____	$_____	$_____
Foundations	$_____	$_____	$_____	$_____	$_____	$_____
Special events	$_____	$_____	$_____	$_____	$_____	$_____
Cultivation and relationship building	$_____	$_____	$_____	$_____	$_____	$_____
Stewardship activities	$_____	$_____	$_____	$_____	$_____	$_____
Total	$_____	$_____	$_____	$_____	$_____	$_____
IN-KIND	$_____	$_____	$_____	$_____	$_____	$_____

Give examples of types of in-kind donations you accept

HOW DO THE RESULTS COMPARE WITH WHAT WAS BUDGETED FOR FUNDRAISING IN EACH YEAR?

Budgeted	$_____	$_____	$_____	$_____	$_____	$_____
Realized	$_____	$_____	$_____	$_____	$_____	$_____
Percentage	$_____	$_____	$_____	$_____	$_____	$_____

B. Budget or cash flow timeline

- Working from the current year's fundraising goals, timeline for implementation, and expense budget, complete the Projected Income and Expenses form, writing in the years at the column heads.

- Looking at the fiscal year for which your organization has the most complete figures, in what month did the development program reach the break-even point? Looking at the current fiscal year, in what month is the development program projected to reach the break-even point? Use the Month-by-Month Analysis of Income and Expenses form provided here or create a similar form.

C. Donor profile

- Evaluate your organization's individual donor base by gift levels. Use the Individual Donors by Gift Level, by Category, and by Relationship form provided, writing in the years at the column heads, and adjusting it for relevance to your organization.

D. Prospect pool profile

- Determine the total pool of donor and nondonor names on which your organization can draw, by prospect categories and relationships. Use the Total Prospect Pool by Category and by Relationship form provided, writing in the years at the column heads, and adjusting it for relevance to your organization.

E. Donor demographic profile

- Provide a demographic data analysis of your organization's donor base. If you are unable to get this information from your computer, then create an analysis of your organization's top 100 donors, using the Analysis of Demographic Data for Top 100 Donors form provided here.

SAMPLE FORM: PROJECTED INCOME AND EXPENSES

	Year _____	Year _____	Year _____
Total income projected	$_____	$_____	$_____
Total expenses projected	$_____	$_____	$_____
Net income projected	$_____	$_____	$_____
Ratio of income to expenses	$_____	$_____	$_____

SAMPLE FORM: MONTH-BY-MONTH ANALYSIS OF INCOME AND EXPENSES

	Month 1	Month 2	Month 3	Month 4	Month 5
EXPENSES					
Computer	$_____	$_____	$_____	$_____	$_____
Gift acknowledgment	$_____	$_____	$_____	$_____	$_____
Staffing	$_____	$_____	$_____	$_____	$_____
Direct fundraising					
Major	$_____	$_____	$_____	$_____	$_____
Annual	$_____	$_____	$_____	$_____	$_____
Mail	$_____	$_____	$_____	$_____	$_____
Newsletter	$_____	$_____	$_____	$_____	$_____
Phone	$_____	$_____	$_____	$_____	$_____
Events	$_____	$_____	$_____	$_____	$_____
Cultivation	$_____	$_____	$_____	$_____	$_____
Stewardship	$_____	$_____	$_____	$_____	$_____
Total expenses	$_____	$_____	$_____	$_____	$_____
INCOME					
Direct fundraising					
Major	$_____	$_____	$_____	$_____	$_____
Annual	$_____	$_____	$_____	$_____	$_____
Mail	$_____	$_____	$_____	$_____	$_____
Newsletter	$_____	$_____	$_____	$_____	$_____
Phone	$_____	$_____	$_____	$_____	$_____
Events	$_____	$_____	$_____	$_____	$_____
Total income	$_____	$_____	$_____	$_____	$_____
CASH FLOW					
Monthly	$_____	$_____	$_____	$_____	$_____
Accrued	$_____	$_____	$_____	$_____	$_____

SAMPLE FORM: INDIVIDUAL DONORS BY GIFT LEVEL, BY CATEGORY, AND BY RELATIONSHIP

	Number of Donors in _____ (Year)	Number of Donors in _____ (Year)	Number of Donors in _____ (Year)
TOTAL NUMBER OF DONORS	_____	_____	_____
DONORS BY GIFT LEVEL			
$1 million or more	_____	_____	_____
$500,000–$999,999	_____	_____	_____
$100,000–$499,000	_____	_____	_____
$50,000–$99,999	_____	_____	_____
$10,000–$49,999	_____	_____	_____
$1,000–$9,999	_____	_____	_____
$750–$999	_____	_____	_____
$500–$749	_____	_____	_____
$250–$499	_____	_____	_____
$100–$249	_____	_____	_____
$50–$99	_____	_____	_____
$25–$49	_____	_____	_____
Under $25	_____	_____	_____
DONORS BY CATEGORY			
Annual giving	_____	_____	_____
Direct mail	_____	_____	_____
Phone-a-thon	_____	_____	_____
Face-to-face	_____	_____	_____
Major giving	_____	_____	_____
Planned giving	_____	_____	_____
Realized bequests	_____	_____	_____
New expectancies	_____	_____	_____
Special events	_____	_____	_____
In-kind	_____	_____	_____
Corporate	_____	_____	_____
Foundations	_____	_____	_____
DONORS BY RELATIONSHIP			
Board members	_____	_____	_____
Staff or faculty	_____	_____	_____
Family of clients	_____	_____	_____
Friends	_____	_____	_____

SAMPLE FORM: TOTAL PROSPECT POOL BY CATEGORY AND BY RELATIONSHIP

	Number of Prospects in ____ (Year)	Number of Prospects in ____ (Year)	Number of Prospects in ____ (Year)
TOTAL NUMBER OF PROSPECTS	_____	_____	_____
PROSPECTS BY CATEGORY			
Annual giving	_____	_____	_____
Direct mail	_____	_____	_____
Phone-a-thon	_____	_____	_____
Face-to-face	_____	_____	_____
Major giving	_____	_____	_____
Planned giving	_____	_____	_____
Corporate	_____	_____	_____
Foundations	_____	_____	_____
Total prospects by category	_____	_____	_____
PROSPECTS BY RELATIONSHIP			
Board members	_____	_____	_____
Staff	_____	_____	_____
Family of clients	_____	_____	_____
Friends	_____	_____	_____
Total prospects by relationship	_____	_____	_____

F.   Overall fundraising strategy

Key Questions to Answer

- Where can dollars potentially come from?
- In what form are these potential dollars? Cash? Volunteer help? Sponsorships? Gifts in kind?
- Are there (realistic) major funders? Individuals? Foundations? Corporations?
- What input has your organization used in determining fundraising goals? Board input? Staff input? Volunteer input? Community input?

- Provide a spreadsheet showing all your organization's fundraising activities, month by month, for the last complete fiscal year. Also provide a spreadsheet showing completed activities and anticipated activities for the current year.

SAMPLE FORM: ANALYSIS OF DEMOGRAPHIC DATA FOR TOP 100 DONORS

	Total Number of Donors	Under 40 Years of Age	40 to 50 Years of Age	Over 55 Years of Age
BY GENDER				
Male	_____	_____	_____	_____
Female	_____	_____	_____	_____
BY RACE OR ETHNICITY				
White, non-Hispanic	_____	_____	_____	_____
African American	_____	_____	_____	_____
Hispanic	_____	_____	_____	_____
Asian	_____	_____	_____	_____
Native American	_____	_____	_____	_____
BY HOUSEHOLD				
Single	_____	_____		_____
Married	_____	_____		_____
BY INCOME				
Under $50,000	_____	_____	_____	_____
$50,000–$75,000	_____	_____	_____	_____
Over $100,000	_____	_____	_____	_____

	Total $$ Raised	Annual Gifts	Major Gifts	Bequests and Life Income Gifts (Expectancies and Realized)
BY AGE				
Under 40 Years	$_____	$_____	$_____	$_____
40–50 Years	$_____	$_____	$_____	$_____
Over 55 Years	$_____	$_____	$_____	$_____
BY GENDER				
Male	$_____	$_____	$_____	$_____
Female	$_____	$_____	$_____	$_____
BY RACE OR ETHNICITY				
White, non-Hispanic	$_____	$_____	$_____	$_____
African American	$_____	$_____	$_____	$_____
Hispanic	$_____	$_____	$_____	$_____
Asian	$_____	$_____	$_____	$_____
Native American	$_____	$_____	$_____	$_____
BY HOUSEHOLD				
Single	$_____	$_____	$_____	$_____
Married	$_____	$_____	$_____	$_____
BY INCOME				
Under $50,000	$_____	$_____	$_____	$_____
$50,000–$75,000	$_____	$_____	$_____	$_____
$75,000–$100,000	$_____	$_____	$_____	$_____
Over $100,000	$_____	$_____	$_____	$_____

- Provide copies of all communications and fundraising materials including the following:

  Annual report

  Newsletter(s)

  Letters from the executive director and the board chair

  Public service announcements and paid media ads

  Gift recognition levels brochure

  Planned giving brochure

  Follow-up planned giving brochure

  Scholarship brochure

  Tribute and memorial brochure

  Wish list brochure (examples of needs)

  Corporate giving brochure

G. Computerization

  - Is your organization computerized for fundraising?

  - Does it have a software package that tracks donors and their donations?

  - If your organization does have a software package, what system does it use? Provide documentation and copies of screens.

  - How sophisticated is this system? Can it find and sort by a variety of demographics? Can it personalize communications?

  - Evaluate how user friendly this system is by answering these questions:

    Is it fast?

    Is it flexible in its coding classifications?

    Does it have a proven track record among not-for-profits?

    Does the vendor provide ongoing support, via phone, at a reasonable cost?

    Are enhancements provided free or at a modest cost?

    Can it acknowledge linked gifts of couples, and not attribute the gift to just one person?

H. Stewardship and accountability

  - Does your organization have guidelines for gift stewardship? Do the guidelines answer these questions?

    What kinds of gifts does your organization accept?

    At what level may donors restrict their gifts?

    What kinds of donor acknowledgment and recognition are provided?

Is your organization gender sensitive, acknowledging both members of a couple when both give; that is, is it recognizing each as an individual? (Do donor records have the married women's names recorded in the form they prefer?)

Who at your organization may accept gifts?

How are in-kind gifts valued for recognition?

How are operating costs and fundraising costs recovered from restricted or endowment gifts?

What level of funding does your organization require for endowments? For facility namings? For the customary forms of planned gifts?

I. Gift acknowledgment and recognition

- How does your organization handle gift acknowledgments? Does your organization use a standard gift reply form? Provide samples of all reply forms. What is the dollar cutoff level for sending each type of acknowledgment?

- Using the following form, determine how long it takes your organization to send acknowledgments to donors. If the time is longer than ideal, why does it take this long?

Length of Time	Normally	Peak Periods
Within 1 week (ideal)	_____	_____
Within 2 weeks (acceptable)	_____	_____
Longer (problematic)	_____	_____

- What forms of donor recognition does your organization have? Use the following list. (Check all that apply.) Provide samples of relevant materials; explain when they are used and for whom.

___Annual honor roll

___Plaques, certificates

___Articles in newsletter

___Thank-you calls from board or staff members

___Donor events

___Donor clubs and recognition societies

How does your organization recruit members for these groups?

How does your organization get members to upgrade?

Does your organization include both spouses as members? Does it recognize couples by listing the first names of both?

J. Fundraising methodologies

1. Major (individual) gifts

Key Questions to Answer

- What is the ability of staff to do each stage of the major gift development cycle and involve other key staff members and volunteers at important times?
- What access do staff have to prospects; what ability to meet with them?
- Does the organization give staff adequate encouragement through frequent meetings, computer-supported reminder systems, and a good evaluation process that stresses relationship building?

- What constitutes a major gift donor? Use the following list. (Check all that apply.)

    ___Size of gift

    ___Frequency of giving

    ___Recency of gift

    ___Cumulative size of gifts

    ___Number of years of giving

- Who are your organization's current major donors and prospects?
- What kinds of research does your organization do on major gift donors and prospects? Use the following list. (Check all that apply.) Provide an explanation of each type of research done.

    ___Sends donor surveys out regularly.

    ___Researches spouses of current givers.

    ___Prioritizes existing donors to identify the best prospects. (Criteria might include size of gifts, frequency of giving, cumulative giving.)

    ___Uses philanthropic records of other organizations to identify donors who are making fair share gifts to your organization but more significant gifts elsewhere.

    ___Uses public records (announcements of promotions, lists of inside stock trades, books of lists, and so forth) to identify levels of affluence.

    ___Uses donor screening packages to identify levels of affluence.

    ___Uses databases and research materials. Which databases and materials does your organization have? Provide a list. Which does it use regularly?

- Once you know your organization's major gift donors and prospects, the next stages in major gift work are relationship building, motivating, asking, acknowledging, and providing stewardship. Provide a detailed narrative to answer each of the following questions:

What strategies is your organization using to build relationships with current and future major gift donors? Does it use one-on-one visits with donors? Site visits? Cultivation and stewardship events, such as personal recognition in the form of lunch with the executive director or CEO? Other strategies (describe them)? Are staff involved in stewardship of gifts? Do they create reports for donors or gather such information?

How are organizational staff trained for making major gift calls? There are four steps in major gift work: identify (cold call) prospects, build relationships with them, motivate them, and ask for major gifts. Analyze each staff member in terms of his or her communication skills in working with major donors one-on-one in each step. Are some staff better at relationship building and some better at asking for the gift?

Are staff comfortable visiting donors in any setting? Are they visiting couples and individual men and women in equal numbers or in relation to their frequency as donors? (Some organizations will find their donor base is primarily women but the major gift staff are visiting mainly men.)

What types of major donor cultivation, informational, and relationship-building events does your organization hold? How often are they held?

What kind of system does your organization have to assist development staff in visiting and continuing relationships with major donors (prospect tracking)?

What is the executive director's attitude toward major gift visits? Does the director prefer the role of identifier, relationship builder, motivator, asker, or steward? Does the director take on more than one role?

Does your organization have a routine evaluation process for reviewing the technique of the executive director in working with major donors?

What measures are used to evaluate major gift development staff? Are they evaluated by number of relationships? Number of visits? Amount of money raised? Other measures (describe them)?

What is your organization's major gift prospect assignment or access policy? That is, who determines who can see whom? Can any staff member visit any prospect or donor as long as he or she checks with staff who have already had contact with that person? Is there a gatekeeper function? Does the executive director let Development Office staff visit the top prospects?

What kind of internal communication is required for major gifts? Is about the same amount of time given to major gift reporting and to reviewing the top prospects as is given to reviewing the details of the annual fund? Do all staff members know who the top 100 donors and prospects are?

Is there a computerized communication system where staff record contacts with donors and send electronic copies to colleagues?

How many major prospects are assigned to each major gift staff member? What is the number of people each staff person is expected to communicate with each year? How many of the donors or prospects in each gift category does each staff person manage?

How often does the director of development meet with major gift staff to assess progress with donors or prospects and discuss activity with the top twenty prospects?

2. Planned giving

    - Define what constitutes a planned gift donor. Identify the types of gifts and the size of gifts.

    - Who are your organization's current planned donors and prospects?

    - What kinds of research does your organization do on planned gift donors and prospects? Use the following list. (Check all that apply.) Provide an explanation of each type of research done.

      ___Sends out donor surveys regularly.

      ___Researches spouses of current givers.

      ___Prioritizes existing donors to identify the best prospects. (Criteria might include size of gifts, frequency of giving, cumulative giving.)

      ___Uses philanthropic records of other organizations to identify donors who are making fair share gifts to your organization but more significant gifts elsewhere.

      ___Uses public records (announcements of promotions, lists of inside stock trades, books of lists, and so forth) to identify levels of affluence.

___Uses donor screening packages to identify levels of affluence.

___Uses databases and research materials. (Which databases and materials does your organization have? Provide a list. Which does it use regularly?)

- Once you know your organization's planned donors and prospects, the next stages in planned gift work are relationship building, motivating, asking, acknowledging, and providing stewardship. Provide a detailed narrative to answer each of the following questions:

What strategies are your staff using to build relationships with current and future planned gift donors? Are they using one-on-one visits with donors? Site visits? Cultivation and stewardship events, such as personal recognition in the form of lunch with the executive director or CEO? Other measures (describe them)?

How are your staff trained for making planned gift calls? There are four steps in planned gift work: identify (cold call) prospects, build relationships with them, motivate them, and ask for or offer stewardship for planned gifts. Analyze each staff member in terms of his or her communication skills in working with planned gift donors one-on-one in each step. Are some staff better at relationship building and some better at asking for the gift?

Are staff comfortable with visiting donors in any setting? Are they visiting couples and individual men and women in equal numbers or in relation to their frequency as donors? (Again, organizations may find their prospects for planned giving are primarily women and their planned gift staff are visiting mainly men.)

What types of planned gift donor cultivation, informational, and relationship-building events does your organization hold? How often are they held?

Does your organization use any of the following in planned gift donor cultivation? (Check all that apply.) Provide copies.

___Brochures

___Financial planning mailings

___Articles in newsletter

___Mailings

___Advertisements

___Recognition vehicles

How does your organization handle inquiries?

Does it have an advisory council of planned gift professionals (for example, estate attorneys, financial planners, bank trust offices)?

List all advisory council members or provide their biographies.

Describe the council function and its meeting schedule.

Does your organization hold planned giving seminars and workshops? Provide invitations, brochures, and other literature.

What kind of system does your organization have to assist development staff in visiting and continuing relationships with planned donors (prospect tracking)?

Does your organization track expectancies? If it does, how are they tracked? Provide a list of expectancies.

What is the executive director's attitude toward planned gift visits? Does the director prefer the role of identifier, relationship builder, motivator, asker, or steward? Does the director take on more than one role?

Does your organization have a routine evaluation process for reviewing the technique of the executive director in working with planned donors?

What measures are used to evaluate planned gift development staff? Are they evaluated by number of relationships? Number of visits? Amount of money raised? Other measures (describe them)?

What is your organization's planned gift prospect assignment or access policy? That is, who determines who can see whom? Can any staff member visit any prospect or donor as long as he or she checks with staff who have already had contact with that person? Is there a gatekeeper function? Does the executive director let Development Office staff visit the top prospects?

What kind of internal communication is required for planned gifts? Is about the same amount of time given to planned gift reporting and reviewing of the top prospects as is given to reviewing the details of the annual fund? Do all staff members know who the top 100 donors and prospects are?

Is there a computerized communication system where staff record contacts with planned gift prospects and send electronic copies to colleagues?

How many planned gift prospects are assigned to each planned gift staff member? What is the number of people each staff person is expected to communicate with each year? How many of the donors or prospects in each category does each staff person manage?

How often does the director of development meet with planned gift staff to assess progress with donors or prospects and discuss activity with the top twenty prospects?

3. Annual fundraising

- Define an *annual donor.*

- Compare your organization's past two complete fiscal years in terms of annual fundraising. Use the following form, writing in the years at the column heads.

	Year ____	Year ____
Total number of annual donors	_____	_____
Number of renewing donors	_____	_____
$$ from renewing donors	_____	_____
Number of new donors	_____	_____
$$ from new donors	_____	_____

- What percentage of your organization's annual donors renewed their gifts from the previous fiscal year?

- What percentage of your organization's annual donors renewed and upgraded their gifts?

- Does your organization have a formally structured annual giving program with defined timelines and steps? If it does, provide documentation.

- Describe the audience with which each of the following methodologies is used.

  In-person solicitation

  Direct mail

  Telemarketing and telecommunications

- Does your organization benefit from matching gifts? What is the annual dollar amount? How many matching gift donors does the organization have? How does it promote matching gifts?

- What themes, if any, does your organization use? Use the following list. (Check all that apply.)

  ___Early giving

  ___End-of-year giving

  ___End-of-fiscal-year giving

  ___Financial aid or scholarship appeal

  ___Tribute or memorial giving

  ___Facilities needs

  ___Crisis appeal

- Does your organization differentiate between renewal and acquisition fundraising? Describe the strategy used for each. Who are the audiences? What vehicles are used? What is the timing?

4.   Corporate and foundation giving

   - Compile a list (going back up to three years) of your organization's corporate and foundation funders. What was the area of support in each case? What was the size of gift(s) received?

   - Has your organization developed and rated a significant prospect list?

   - Does your organization have a formal strategy for moving corporate and foundation prospects along? Provide documentation.

   - How does your organization communicate opportunities to apply for grants to program staff? Does it use a newsletter (provide a copy)? Meetings? Informal methods?

   - Does your organization do prospect research on a regular basis? How is this research accomplished?

   - Does your organization have updated lists of corporations and foundations and their giving policies and histories? When did staff last ask for this information?

   - What local, regional, and national resources do you have in the Development Office? Use the following list. (Check all that apply.)

     ___Membership in the Foundation Center

     ___Publications (list all you have; include publication date)

     ___*Corporate and Foundation Givers* and *Prospector's Choice,* profiling corporate and foundation grantmakers, from the Taft Group

     ___*Chronicle Guide to Grants,* from the Chronicle of Higher Education

     ___Foundation Center directories

     ___A local foundation directory

5.   Special events

Key Questions to Answer

- Does your organization define event objectives? Which events are income producing? Friend raising? Designed to cultivate major donors and emphasize gift stewardship?

- Does your organization fully track special event expenses, including in-kind and time?

- Does your organization have a particular event or events held each year?

  Provide a description of each event, including the dollar amount raised, who attends, the number attending, the budget, who runs the event, and so forth.

  For each event that has taken place two or more times, compare expense and income year-by-year.

  Classify each event as one of the following:

  > *Rising star.* Encourage growth to the logical maximum for events that produce increasing income, with even higher future potential. Put additional resources behind these events. They are likely to be aimed at baby boomer audiences.

  > *Problem child.* Consider the potential of these events for *friend raising* instead of *fundraising.* An event that doesn't make much sense in terms of the dollars it generates may be very important in another context. Events aimed at special audiences (perhaps women or people of color) often fall into this category.

  > *Cash cow.* Can the organization maintain the dollars currently being achieved from these events without increasing staff involvement or expenses? Cash cows can often become largely the responsibility of volunteers working under a well thought out *contract* of responsibilities. Many of the events that do well with traditional mature audiences are cash cows.

  > *Dog.* Discontinue these events as quickly as possible. Cash cows can deteriorate into dogs without warning. Signs of new dogs include slowing growth and increasing expenses. Golf outings and other physically intensive events may become dogs quickly.

6. Other fundraising income

   - Provide any information that might be useful about other fundraising income (for example, income from product sales).

K. Fundraising staffing

1. Job descriptions

   - Provide the names and titles of all development professional and support staff for the current year and provide a job description and résumé for each.

   - How accurate are these job descriptions when compared to individuals' actual responsibilities?

2. Organizational chart

   • Provide the organizational or reporting charts for the Development Office (for the last three years, if available).

3. Director of development

   (This section is to be completed by the director of development.)

   • For each area on the following list, indicate whether you have direct responsibility, supervisory responsibility, or passive involvement.

   Direct fundraising

   Face-to-face cultivation and solicitation, either on your own or with board members or staff (in this activity, do you prefer the role of identifier, relationship-builder, motivator, asker, or steward, or are you active in more than one stage?)

   Oversight of staff on prospect assignments and review of their major gift calls

   Fundraising or cultivation events

   Grant writing

   Preparing brochures and letters

   Support activities

   Meetings with the board, committees, and staff

   Report generation

   Data entry

   Record keeping

   Gift acknowledgment

   Stewardship reporting to donors

   Other non-fundraising activities (describe them)

4. Other professional development staff

   • For each area on the following list, indicate whether professional development staff other than the director of development have direct responsibility, supervisory responsibility, or passive involvement.

   Direct fundraising

   Face-to-face cultivation and solicitation either on one's own or with board members or staff

   Fundraising or cultivation events

Grant writing

Preparing brochures and letters

Stewardship reporting to donors

Support activities

Meetings with board, committees, and staff

Report generation

Data entry

Record keeping

Gift acknowledgment

Other non-fundraising activities (describe them)

- How does the Development Office interact with the rest of the organization?

Who from the Development Office attends management meetings?

Who attends board meetings?

How does the Development Office learn about programs?

How early do development staff get information?

5. Support staff

- For each area on the following list, indicate whether development support staff have direct responsibility, supervisory responsibility, or passive involvement.

Direct fundraising

Face-to-face cultivation and solicitation either on one's own or with board members or staff

Fundraising or cultivation events

Grant writing

Preparing brochures and letters

Stewardship reporting to donors

Support activities

Meetings with board, committees, and staff

Report generation

Data entry

Record keeping

Gift acknowledgment

Other non-fundraising activities (describe them)

- How do development support staff interact with the rest of the organization?

  Who from development support staff attends management meetings?

  Who attends board meetings?

  How do development support staff learn about programs?

  How early do development support staff get information?

L. Fundraising resources

Key Questions to Answer

- Do development staff have ready access to up-to-date resources?
- Do development staff have an understanding of the resources that are available?
- Do development staff use outside resources?

---

1. Professional growth opportunities

    - What professional memberships do staff have?

    - What professional meetings do staff attend? Do they attend regularly? Infrequently?

    - What training events have staff attended in the last three years? List both internal and external events.

    - What training is scheduled for staff for this year? For next year? List both internal and external events.

2. Resource library

    - What general publications do Development Office staff regularly receive and read?

    - What subscriptions to local paper and business papers does the office have? What parts of the newspapers do staff review? Do they look at the society or social pages? Insider trading? People on the move?

    - What fundraising publications do Development Office staff regularly receive and read? Use the following list. (Check all that apply.)

      ____*The Chronicle of Philanthropy*

      ____*Fund Raising Management* magazine

____*The Nonprofit Times*

____*Contributions* magazine

____*Advancing Philanthropy*—the NSFRE Journal

____Other specialized publications and newsletters (provide a list)

- What books on fundraising are available in house for staff? Provide a list.

3. Idea generation

- How do Development Office staff share ideas?

  Formally: Regular staff meetings? Retreats?

  Informally: Lunch together? Hallway meetings?

IV. PUBLIC RELATIONS, IMAGE, OUTREACH

Key Questions to Answer

- How well does your organization's public relations function support the organization's main program and fundraising objectives?

  Crisis management. Does it respond in a logical manner to control damage to the organization's reputation resulting from internal concerns or from public perceptions of concerns?

  Public information. Does it respond quickly to the public's need for information and desire to help?

  Leadership positioning. Does it work to solidify the community's perception of the organization as the best not-for-profit in its area?

  Fund and friend raising. Does it raise the organization from a fair share not-for-profit to a priority one for donors and volunteers?

A. The view from outside

- How well do others understand your organization's mission, goals, and objectives?

- How is your organization viewed by peer organizations? How is it viewed by the legislature? By the broader community locally? Regionally? Nationally?

- Which of the following view your organization as a leader? Use the following list. (Check all that apply.)

    ___Other area not-for-profits and United Way

    ___Community leaders not associated with your organization

    ___Board members and other volunteers

    ___Clients and their families

    ___Donors

    ___Staff

B. Media resources

- How is your organization's image influenced?

    What media resources in your community does your organization use? Does it use newspapers? Radio stations? Television stations? Alternative media? Minority outreach media?

    What community, workplace, and company outreach vehicles does your organization use? Does it use library and church bulletin boards? Other not-for-profit organizations? Company newsletters? Volunteer coordinators?

    How does your organization communicate with each of the media and vehicles available to it? When do staff communicate with these resources (on an ongoing basis or mainly at times of crisis)?

    What outreach events does your organization schedule? Does it have a speakers bureau? Does it schedule focus groups? Recognition events? Open houses? Other events (describe them)?

V. ADDITIONAL INFORMATION

Add any information that is appropriate. This might include information about membership and product items.

Part Four

The Development Assessment in Action

Chapter 8

How One Organization Used Development Assessment to Strengthen Fundraising Programs: A Case Example

THE DEVELOPMENT ASSESSMENT REPORT puts the answers gathered from all the resources into a framework that is persuasive because it is as logical and as nonthreatening as possible.

The report example used in this chapter concerns a multifaceted human service provider (the "ABC Organization") located in Portland, Oregon. Part of a national organization, it has served its local community for more than one hundred years with a variety of programs for the elderly, individuals in crisis, families, and children. ABC's fundraising results—although steady—now lack the more spectacular gains of previous years. In deciding to do a development assessment, the leadership and board acknowledged they thought there was cause for concern. The assessment report's findings and recommendations were shared with ABC's board, general staff, and development staff and were used for a major reorganization of the ABC Office of Development.

Although each assessment must be addressed to the unique strengths and concerns of the particular not-for-profit, development assessment reports in general have many similarities in structure. You are encouraged to use the case example on the following pages as a jumping-off point; you are welcome to use as much of the material as works for you as is, but do not hesitate to improve on what you read. There is no one right or wrong way of organizing the material, but over many years of doing assessments, I have found that proceeding from the general to the specific seems to work best.

A Proposed Development Strategy for the ABC Organization

Prepared and submitted by Judith E. Nichols, Ph.D., CFRE

Table of Contents

Introduction

Executive Summary

Developing the Case for Support

- Does ABC Have Credibility with the Public?
- Is There a Rationale for Raising More Private Dollars?
  - Defining the Need
  - Interpreting the Need in Dollars
- Can ABC Attract Increased Private Support?
  - Defining the Positive Indicators
  - Defining the Concerns

Moving to the New Paradigm

- Addressing Organizational Issues
- Strengthening Board Leadership in Development
  - Helping Board Members Understand Responsibilities
  - Setting and Approving Development Goals and Objectives
  - Developing Gift Stewardship and Accountability Guidelines
  - Determining the Fundraising Role of the Executive Director
- Reorganizing the Development Office
  - Computerizing
  - Making the Budget Commitment
  - Evaluating Current and Future Fundraising Methodologies
  - Evaluating Fundraising Staff

The Proposed Development Strategy

- Moving from a Broad-Based to a Focused Development Strategy
- Increasing Community Understanding of ABC
- Increasing Results by Strengthening the Individual Fundraising Components
    - Major Giving
    - Planned Giving
    - Annual Giving
    - Special Events
    - Corporate and Foundation Relations

Recommended Steps for Implementation: Timeline

Resources: Supporting Materials

- Resource A: Responsibilities of the Board (Sample Job Description)
- Resource B: Sample Gift Stewardship and Accountability Guidelines

Appendixes

- Appendix A: Program and Service Needs Assessment Results
- Appendix B: List of Participants
- Appendix C: List of Materials Requested and Gathered
- Appendix D: Copy of the Development Assessment Survey

Introduction

Change is inevitable and nonnegotiable, presenting both opportunities and challenges. Although it can be threatening, disruptive, and anxiety provoking, change is also transforming, revitalizing, and energizing. Organizations have several options for dealing with change:

- Ignore it and chance death.
- Study trends and adjust to them.
- Anticipate events and move first.
- Lead and make things happen.

Unfortunately, too often, change takes not-for-profits unaware. Then they play catch-up: trying desperately to move to the new reality. To address new paradigms, not-for-profits must understand what today's and tomorrow's realities are.

This report is a summary of the findings of a development assessment conducted by Judith E. Nichols for the ABC Organization, January through March 1997. The goal is to provide the ABC Organization with an understanding of what it can do to restructure its fundraising to support the goals and objectives it will carry into the next century. The purpose of the development assessment is to position ABC to maximize its fund development efforts. The assessment does this by

- Evaluating what is currently being done by the ABC Organization

- Realistically assessing the potential for raising money from different audiences

- Suggesting strategy steps and tools to help the organization get from where it is to where it needs to be, quickly and cost effectively

The findings and recommendations in this report are based on information gathered by an assessment survey, a review of internal materials and relevant external materials, and meetings held with the individuals involved both directly and indirectly in fundraising for the ABC Organization. By opening up a dialogue among key players and structuring information gathering for more accurate decision making, the development assessment encourages buy-in by staff and volunteers.

The assessment report begins with an analysis of all the data gathered on ABC's organizational and fundraising history. It then provides a pragmatic analysis of the current development strategy, defining the key areas of concern, identifying the roles of volunteers and staff, defining the priorities for implementation, and creating a timeline for achievement within the context of realistic, yet challenging, goal setting. Again, the goal is to give the ABC Organization the tools to position its fundraising so as to achieve the greatest potential results.

This development assessment helps to answer the following questions:

- How well thought out are ABC's fundraising goals?

- How committed are ABC's leadership and volunteers to achieving fundraising success?

- Does ABC have a constituency base that is able and willing to respond to those needs?

- Does ABC have the resources needed to carry out development objectives successfully?

- How competent and prepared are ABC's staff and volunteers?

- Where is ABC today and what is it selling to the public? What is it selling to its donors?

- Is what ABC is today what it wants to be tomorrow?

- Do ABC's potential public perceive ABC in the same manner its people perceive it?

- Do the public, by and large, approve of ABC's work and endorse its objectives for tomorrow?

- What kinds of financial resources will ABC need to finance the objectives it has in mind for tomorrow?

- What are ABC's financial priorities in everything from construction to program needs?

- Are the people in ABC behind the organization's vision and do they understand the goals ahead?

- With whom is ABC competing? Is there anything particularly unique or distinctive about ABC's approach to the field?

- How does ABC best communicate its distinctions, goals, and objectives to its public?

- Where do ABC's board members and volunteers fit into the development process?

- How do the roles of the executive director and other key administrators, board members, development and other staff, and volunteers complement each other in the development process?

This written report on the development assessment is organized as follows:

The executive summary summarizes the main points of the report for quick reference, including the rationales and recommendations.

"Developing the Case for Support" presents the background information upon which the analysis with its conclusions and recommendations rests, describing how well positioned ABC is to raise money. This section looks at *the rationale for raising more private support:* What are the reasons for asking for additional donor commitments? What are the anticipated needs currently, in the near future, and looking further out? How much will various operating, capital, and endowment needs cost? This section also looks at whether ABC can *attract increased private support:* Who are ABC's current donors? Are they able to increase their support? And, looking at both the demographic and the psychographic information, is there a logical new pool of donors to attract?

In addition, this section discusses specific areas of concern in detail: Does the community understand the ABC Organization's mission? Does ABC's leadership understand the role of development in the organization's success? Is there development leadership from staff and key volunteers? Is there a cohesive development strategy?

"Moving to the New Paradigm" is concerned with organizational restructuring issues, how well the board is organized for its fundraising responsibilities, and the status of the development office.

The section titled "The Proposed Development Strategy" discusses the overall recommended strategy, steps for goal setting, and the specifics of fundraising. Each area of a full development program is outlined.

"Recommended Steps for Implementation" summarizes the timeline necessary for moving to the new strategy.

"Resources: Supporting Materials" offers additional information on and explanations for recommended strategic steps concerning both board and donor development.

The appendixes contain data from the needs assessment, a list of those who provided input to the assessment process, a summary of the materials requested and gathered, and a copy of the development assessment survey.

Each assessment offers its own unique challenges. Information gathering was particularly difficult in this case. Although individuals were willing to cooperate, the requested materials were often not available. Comparisons from year to year were difficult because the criteria underlying data gathering in previous years had changed frequently. For these reasons, specifics should be looked at cautiously.

However, the conclusions are—I firmly believe—accurate and useful to the ABC Organization.

Executive Summary

Currently the fundraising at the ABC Organization is far below its potential. When inflation is taken into account, private support is down. Compared to comparable community organizations, the ABC organization is losing ground rapidly.

Increased support for an organization can occur only

- *When the organization is viewed as competent, with strong leadership and a solid mission.* This means

  There is a clear vision, developed and agreed upon by the organization's leadership, of what the organization is and why it is important to its community.

  The dollar costs of funding organizational goals and objectives have been quantified.

  There is a dedicated and trained group of board members and volunteers committed to serving as the organization's advocates in fundraising.

- *When the organization is receptive to private support.* This means

  There is a logical base of prospects who are financially capable of supporting the organization's goals and objectives.

  There is a willingness to commit the necessary resources to cultivate the organization's prospects and grow its donors.

  The organization accepts its responsibility to provide stewardship and accountability.

Once these key elements are in place

- *Then the organization must choose a model for its fundraising that fits its culture, strengths, and areas of concern.*

  There must be a well thought out, prioritized fundraising strategy that challenges and energizes supporters.

  There must be commitment to providing the resources to carry out the strategy within a realistic, yet challenging time frame.

To realistically determine whether and how the ABC Organization can successfully increase its share of private support, each of these key necessary elements was evaluated. The overall conclusion is that *the overall economic, philanthropic, and societal trends (including demographic and psychographic analysis of the overall U.S. and specific state populations) provide a window of opportunity for the ABC Organization to dramatically increase its private support.*

The ABC Organization—like many charitable organizations—was formed from the strongly held beliefs of its founders and was supported in its early stages primarily—if not totally—by the deep, often sacrificial commitments of very personally involved individuals. Although organizations with such histories initially find raising money easy because of the strong ties between the organization and its early supporters, they often have problems as they move into maturity. Unfortunately, such organizations often display characteristics that reduce their ability to communicate effectively outside the organizational *family:*

A conscious or unconscious separation of the organization from the rest of the world

A confidence that what is needed will happen of its own accord

An inability to view activities outside the direct delivery of the mission as having worth

The ABC Organization has not organized itself to encourage increased support from outside its family. There are serious issues that it must first address if it is to succeed in attracting additional private support. Here are the key areas of concern:

• Is the ABC Organization "too big to get your arms around"? Too many of ABC's current and potential supporters do not understand the incredible human services outreach of ABC. The vision and mission of the organization as interpreted in programs, projects, and services are not well understood. Although the ABC Organization generally is viewed by the community as necessary and is believed to be both effective and efficient, few of those interviewed could offer specific examples differentiating ABC from other human service providers to support this belief. As a result, when gifts are made, they tend to be modest. Current supporters know that ABC is a good organization. But, being unaware of its many and varied contributions to their communities, they make token or *fair share* donations. The average gift is $11, compared to an average gift at similar organizations of $16 to $25.

ABC's vision must be more clearly articulated to the community. Potential supporters need to be educated about the qualities that distinguish ABC from other philanthropic choices. There is a serious lack of communication, cooperation, and trust between development and other areas of ABC. Top ABC leadership, program directors, volunteers, and development staff must work together in presenting information to the public in the best possible format.

• Fundraising goals are inadequate because they have been based on what ABC has been able to raise in previous years rather than on upcoming funding needs. Although a long-range planning process has been begun, there are serious questions regarding participants' understanding of and commitment to that process. Also, although each program and service area has a general idea of what it wants to accomplish currently, in three to five years, and in five to ten years, there appears to be no formal procedure to ensure that priorities are identified. Based on interviews with the directors of each of the major program and service areas, a starting assessment of needs was made. Each unit was asked to look at three needs:

Operating needs: unrestricted funding for programs and services that are offered on an ongoing basis. Includes staffing and operational costs (rent, materials, and so forth).

Capital needs: restricted funding for specific projects or programs that arise as special needs. Includes facility building and renovation, equipment purchase and upgrading, and so forth, but also is anything that cannot occur without full funding in hand (could be additional staff).

Endowment needs: unrestricted and restricted funding that creates a *safety net* for the organization. Typically recommended as the capital needed to produce 20 percent of the operating needs.

The organizational needs proposed in response to this assessment total significantly more than ABC has probably ever thought itself capable of raising (see the Summary of Fundraising Requirements).

Assuming a more careful analysis bears out dollar figures similar to those shown in the summary, ABC has a strong case for inviting the community to provide additional support. A comprehensive, coordinated development strategy is needed that addresses one-time capital requirements (major giving), operating needs (smaller, annual giving), and endowment (planned giving).

• Private support for the ABC Organization is stagnant (see the Fundraising Income Comparison over Five Years).

ABC ORGANIZATION: SUMMARY OF FUNDRAISING REQUIREMENTS

	Needed Currently	Three to Five Years Out	Five to Ten Years Out
Operating needs	$3,439,909.60	$4,371,875	$5,267,585
Capital needs	344,000.00	13,610,000	9,075,000
Total operating and capital needs	3,783,909.60	17,981,875	14,342,585
Endowment needs	1,000,000.00[a]	6,000,000	15,000,000

[a]Approximately $2,250,000 is currently in endowments and capital trusts.

ABC ORGANIZATION: FUNDRAISING INCOME COMPARISON OVER FIVE YEARS

	FY 1992	FY 1993	FY 1994	FY 1995	FY 1996
Gross income	$1,732,564.28	$1,826,671.11	$2,092,697.11	$2,579,563.11	$2,137,277.98
Direct costs	315,947.23	323,314.23	332,783.51	418,737.34	276,108.19
Net income	1,416,617.05	1,503,356.88	1,759,913.60	2,160,825.77	1,861,169.79
Cost ratio	18.2 percent	17.7 percent	16.0 percent	16.2 percent	13.0 percent

1. Renewal rates are not high enough to provide a stable base of funding and allow ABC to focus efforts on increasing rather than maintaining its levels of private support. Donors are not renewing at a rate of over 60 percent, which is considered the minimum renewal level for maintaining the current level of fundraising. Organizations with superior development programs achieve retention percentage levels in the low nineties.

2. Donors are giving at a level too modest for funding the identified current and future needs. Smaller donors are not being systematically upgraded to committed giving and major gifts. Few gifts over $10,000 are being made to ABC. Fewer than six hundred donors give over $500 annually. This suggests a reverse pyramid: the top tier of donors is contributing 10 percent to 15 percent of the contribution total, as opposed to the 80 percent that is usual in a "healthy" development program. Smaller gifts have a high expense to income ratio and require a high proportion of staff time in relation to the results.

3. When inflation is taken into account, private support is dropping. A comparison of income from direct appeals shows no real increase in the past five years.

4. Compared to comparable community organizations, ABC is losing ground in commanding private support. Conversations with several respected local not-for-profits indicate that many of them—with much smaller potential constituency bases—are raising far more money through annual giving, major gifts, corporate and foundation grants, and expectancies and other planned gifts than the ABC Organization is.

The ABC Organization appears to be raising monies far below its potential. A serious impediment to raising more is the lack of accountability and of well-defined performance evaluation steps. Many of the usual compari-

son reports are not available, and the ones that are available are not consistent in the way information has been gathered by the development staff.

• The ABC Organization needs key volunteers who will *give and get.* Not all ABC board members see fundraising as part of their "contract" with ABC. Newer members have a willingness to both give and get, but they need help: board members' own levels of giving must be challenged, and they must receive training in the skills needed to comfortably ask for money. ABC leadership must form a partnership with these volunteers, providing the *vision* that will support their *endorsement* of ABC. Development staff must do a better job of handling the logistics for the cultivation and solicitation of major gift prospects.

Board members need help in understanding and handling their fundraising responsibilities. A written job description—clearly outlining their "contract" with the organization in terms of both giving and getting—should be developed for use in recruiting new members. Regular training must be provided for board members. Staff must be assigned to help these volunteers with assignments and to track results.

• Current supporters feel no sense of urgency in their giving to ABC. Many donors and prospective supporters assume that the organization has more than enough monies to handle its needs or that "someone else" will step up with the resources.

Talking points, or hooks, must be found that encourage supporters to stretch. They might include a tiered donor recognition program, a menu of large, specific items ABC needs and the gift dollars needed to acquire each of them, and a comprehensive fundraising campaign in conjunction with ABC's upcoming 120th anniversary.

• To reach expanded fundraising goals, ABC must "grow" a pool of younger, more affluent contributors. A review of donor profiles conducted by ABC's direct-mail consulting firm reveals that ABC's traditional donors are aging, and within the next ten to fifteen years, most will be gone. Much of the organization's current and past support has been received from a fairly homogeneous group of donors: they tend to be elderly, white females, with modest incomes and assets. Their main impetus for giving comes from their personal convictions about ABC's well-respected mission.

Midlife adults are going through a reevaluation of values that fits well with the ABC Organization's mission of reaching out to underserved and disadvantaged populations in its community. These prospects are spiritual rather than religious individuals. Compared to ABC's traditional donors, they have different interests, communication styles, payment styles, and expectations in respect to their relationship with the organizations they support. Although ABC is well-positioned to attract this additional pool of donors, doing so will require a new and different approach, including careful segmentation of fundraising materials.

• The ABC Organization must rethink its commitment to development. ABC, like many not-for-profits similar to it, has a culture that requires followers to make a very strong, very personal commitment. Salaries are kept modest; expertise is developed in-house; development functions are often perceived as a necessary nuisance. *Much of ABC's leadership does not understand the role of development and the expertise successful fundraising requires.* ABC needs an organizational commitment to providing the expertise and resources needed to carry out its fundraising.

1. Currently, there is no true head of development. Development staff report to three separate individuals. Most seriously, none of these individuals has a job description specifying the level of responsibility required for efficiently and effectively guiding the development efforts needed to support a quantum leap in ABC's fundraising.

The development operation must be reorganized with a chief development officer (the vice president of development) fully in charge. This individual must have the skills to create, implement, and evaluate all aspects of the program and manage the development staff and volunteers. ABC must be willing to pay for this expertise, with compensation high enough to be competitive with other community organizations.

Current development staff need help in developing the skills needed to carry out the specific strategies. Development is a profession with its own menu of expertise. After conversations with most of the development staff and a review of their résumés, my conclusion is that although a few of them have a good grasp of the areas in which they need expertise, most do not. The necessary expertise must either be grown or hired.

If development staff are to succeed, a regular training program must be implemented. Employees must be encouraged to expand their knowledge through attendance at professional meetings and conferences. A library of reference materials must be made available.

The fundraising staff do not function as a team. Development is not taking place within an atmosphere that encourages trust, communication, coordination, and partnership. Staff do not support each other's efforts or offer each other encouragement. Vital information is not being shared.

The head of the Development Office must make change in this area a priority. Unless there is a positive work environment, gains can not be made. Jobs should be restructured to make better use of personnel resources. Regular staff meetings should be held.

2. A budget must be agreed to that supports an aggressive approach to fundraising. Typically, development costs will run 35 percent to 50 percent in a start-up program; dip to 25 percent to 35 percent during years two through five; and stabilize between 10 percent and 25 percent in maturity. ABC's fundraising cost ratios (cost as a percentage of income raised) are unrealistically low. They are under what I would expect to see in even a mature program, yet ABC's current development program—when compared to its fundraising potential—is still clearly in a start-up phase.

Growing a program requires financial seeding. A realistic development budget must be agreed to. This budget must allow for failure, because only then will it be possible to move to the larger gains. ABC must be willing to make a financial investment for a minimum of three to five years.

ABC's true cost of fundraising is obscured, making comparisons of the development program from one year to the next, difficult. For example, the appeal figures refer only to direct costs (direct-mail production costs, bank charges, postage, and printing), and other costs are scattered among several different fundraising programs. Without adding in all of fundraising's indirect costs (salaries and benefits, office space, and so forth), the cost figures are inaccurate and appear lower than they are.

Finance and development must work together to identify mechanisms to make sure accurate reporting occurs.

There is no accountability. The development staff were unable to produce reports to demonstrate how well their programs were going nor did they appear to feel responsible for any lack of success.

Performance evaluations must be tied to results. Staff must be hired knowing the expectations and must have their progress or lack of it reviewed at regular intervals. New reports must be developed that clearly demonstrate progress or lack of it toward goals.

3. There is no thought-out, long-term development strategy. Rather, the ABC Organization is relying on day-by-day fundraising. To succeed in today's highly competitive fundraising environment, ABC must build upon its strengths and address its areas of concern. Then it must organize its development strategy, prioritizing what it will do and following a timeline

that is both logical and strongly paced. ABC will not be able to accomplish its fundraising goals if it doesn't clearly define those goals. It will go in too many directions and put too much time into programs that bring in only a fraction of the potential possible.

The development strategy must be prioritized. A timeline for implementation needs to be created and agreed to by the executive director, the board, and development staff, with clearly defined goals for performance evaluation.

Conclusion: Overall the ABC Organization *is* well positioned to increase its private support fundraising to cover the operating, capital, and endowment needs of the immediate and longer-term future. ABC possesses the most important characteristic for a strong development program: a highly respected, quality product.

However, ABC has not used its strengths to encourage greater private support. It has an immediate and urgent need to build upon its strong, positive name recognition and other strengths in a logical, organized manner.

To do this, ABC requires a carefully thought out development strategy. It will take at least one year (and more likely, eighteen months) to put in place the framework to support this growth. Once that is done, there should be a rapid and sustained growth in private support.

This assessment will describe how to make that growth happen.

Developing the Case for Support

The mission of the ABC Organization is neither clearly understood nor well articulated. The programs and services that support ABC goals and objectives must be translated into fundraising specifics of operating, capital, and endowment needs and communicated in a style that reaches ABC's best audiences for support.

If the ABC Organization is to raise more money, the public must know the answers to these questions:

Why is ABC unique?

Why is ABC relevant?

What is ABC's impact in the community?

Does ABC Have Credibility with the Public?

How well positioned is the ABC Organization to raise money in relation to specific philanthropic, social, and economic trends?

The ABC Organization through its outreach programs and services is addressing urgent and escalating needs in society, at a time when governments are increasingly stepping back from taking responsibility for those who cannot do so for themselves:

• All segments of our population are living longer. As a result, we are facing a new reality in housing, care-giving, and life-enhancing services for the elderly and those less capable of caring for themselves.

• Our population is diversifying. Immigrants, women, and under-served populations need an advocate they can trust to treat them with dignity and compassion.

• The gap between haves and have-nots is widening, and the gap between these two extremes is becoming harder to bridge.

• Government funding and United Way dollars are not keeping pace with the needs. Vulnerable populations tend to lack an organized political voice and are most susceptible to federal budget cuts.

• The key problems in ABC's community include domestic violence, homelessness among families and children, at-risk youths, and an insufficient number of programs for low-income housing and transitional housing, for drug and alcohol recovery (especially among youths), and for prevention of violence and other problems among youths and families.

The ABC Organization has credibility and demonstrated ability. Within the service provider community, ABC is known and respected for innovation, creativity, and the quality of its programs and services:

• The ABC Organization is well thought of by the community. It has strong name recall nationally; in a recent survey of donors, it was cited by 12 percent of those queried as to which charities they respect. United Ways and churches and other religious organizations were cited by 10 percent. The "DEF Organization" was cited by 8 percent, followed by the "GHI Organization" cited by 3 percent. The "JKL," "MNP," and "QRS" organizations were each cited by 2 percent of the donors.

• The ABC Organization has been a constant presence in this community since 1883. It is the largest single provider of human service programs in the area. In ABC's one hundred–plus years of community service, its integrity and its ability to provide a holistic approach to social concerns and problems have been recognized in the media, by community leaders, and by those benefiting from and supporting its mission.

- The ABC Organization has demonstrated value in terms of the percentage of donated dollars that go to direct service (87 percent).

There must be a broad yet specific vision of what ABC is committed to accomplishing. This vision, in turn, must be clearly articulated as a mission, with a defined menu of programs and services:

- ABC Organization activities in the tricounty area:

   Serves more than 1,000 people each and every day

   Cares for all types of individuals

   Provides a continuum of care through linked programs

- Some 1996 service statistics:

   Unduplicated social work cases served: 8,453

   Nights lodging provided: 39,178

   Meals served: 130,373

   Christmas gifts given: 31,775

- Some 1996 program highlights:

   Adult rehabilitation center: 405 men served; volunteers gave 9,266 hours.

   Camp: 1,266 individuals spent a "week in the woods"; 68 volunteers gave a total of 1,396 hours.

   Family services (five offices): 7,337 (unduplicated) families given food, counseling, and energy utility assistance; 464 volunteers gave a total of 7,975 hours.

   Missing persons services: 602 cases opened; 65 persons located.

   Christmas services: toys, clothes, and food baskets given to 9,235 individuals; 37 volunteers gave a total of 214 hours.

Conclusion: The ABC Organization, both nationally and in Oregon, has strong credibility with the public and an impressive service record. However, in some ways, ABC is "too big to get your arms around."

Those associated with ABC note that the community has a "dated" view of the ABC Organization. Interviewees emphasized that the local community does not understand how ABC serves the greater community. ABC has not taken full advantage of its positive endorsements and credibility when communicating its record to prospects and donors.

Is There a Rationale for Raising More Private Dollars?

Defining the Need

What are the reasons for asking for additional donor commitments?

> *The ABC Organization has been operating all its programs with minimum levels of funding. Unless it has a sizeable influx of private support, it will soon reach a point at which it will have to cut delivery of services severely.*

When ABC's executive director was asked to define ABC's state of economic stability, given choices ranging from stable to recovering from financial crisis, the director named the latter state. For a number of years, ABC has been struggling to recover from debt incurred when it took responsibility for two failing but necessary local charities. ABC's leadership noted that to move the organization into an economic recovery mode, programs have had to cut back drastically on staffing. Staffing is now extremely lean, with positions eliminated or not filled. Many program directors mentioned a strong concern that for ABC to maintain its goal of operating in the black, the leadership would next need to take cuts in services themselves. Given the increasing levels of need in the communities served, along with the cutbacks in state, United Way, and other traditional funding sources, such cuts would weaken ABC's credibility and also severely undermine its mission.

Interpreting the Need in Dollars

> *What are the needs in dollar terms? In order to encourage supporters to rethink their commitment at higher levels, ABC must give current and potential donors an understanding of why ABC should be a charitable priority. What are ABC's anticipated needs currently, in the near future, and looking further out? How much will various operating, capital, and endowment needs cost?*

Like many traditional not-for-profits, the ABC Organization is viewed by many donors as a *fair share* charity, not a giving priority. As a result, few prospects feel an urgency to give at more than token levels.

Fundraising is the end result of a constant cycle of creating donor interest through information, involvement, cultivation, and asking. Fundraising appeals need to make clear the organization's concerns, its leadership role in addressing those concerns, and the gains it has achieved. But the appeals also need to make equally clear the needs that remain. A sense of challenge and urgency needs to be imparted to current and potential supporters to encourage larger annual gifts and create a pool of major and planned gifts.

Conclusion: To encourage donors to give more generously, the ABC Organization needs to present them with a fully articulated package of needs. A full ten-year strategic plan for the organization must be finalized. Discussions with the key ABC board and staff members indicate that the organization's needs are being more fully identified and articulated. A rough assessment, outlined in the accompanying Summary of Fundraising Requirements, should serve in the interim (a program-area-by-program-area breakout appears in Appendix A). This assessment considers needs in three areas:

Operating needs: unrestricted funding for programs and services that are offered on an ongoing basis. Includes staffing and operational costs (rent, materials, and so forth).

Capital needs: restricted funding for specific projects or programs that arise as special needs. Includes facility building and renovation, equipment purchase and upgrading, and so forth, but also is anything that cannot occur without full funding in hand (could be additional staff).

Endowment needs: unrestricted and restricted funding that creates a *safety net* for the organization. Typically recommended as the capital needed to produce 20 percent of the operating needs.

Can ABC Attract Increased Private Support?

Defining the Positive Indicators

• The geographical area's economic indicators are positive. In 1997, per capita income increased 6.2 percent to $21,736, making this state one of the top ten states in income growth for that year. The metro area is experienc-

---

ABC ORGANIZATION: SUMMARY OF FUNDRAISING REQUIREMENTS

	Needed Currently	Three to Five Years Out	Five to Ten Years Out
Operating needs	$3,439,909.60	$4,371,875	$5,267,585
Capital needs	344,000.00	13,610,000	9,075,000
Total operating and capital needs	3,783,909.60	17,981,875	14,342,585
Endowment needs	1,000,000.00[a]	6,000,000	15,000,000

[a]Approximately $2,250,000 is currently in endowments and capital trusts.

ing very robust economic growth, primarily due to high-tech industry expansion.[1] Unemployment is around 3.0 percent. The office vacancy rate is one of the lowest in the nation at 8.2 percent, and the industrial vacancy rate is also one of the lowest in the nation at 1.9 percent.

• ABC's current donor base is heavily weighted with older individuals with *civic* personalities. *This donor base has far surpassed its life expectancy.* Today, many individuals are living well into their eighties, nineties, and beyond. These loyal donors, with their emphasis on "doing the right thing," continue to be a good match with ABC and should be approached for bequests and planned gifts immediately.

• ABC is an excellent match with middle-aged Americans. Boomers (adults born between 1946 and 1964) are the largest adult age group in the United States, constituting 42 percent of the adult population. Many of these middle-aged Americans are reevaluating their lives. And with so many boomers having married later than was once customary or having remarried, record numbers have young children today. Being idealistic by nature, these parents are eager to demonstrate to their children that they are *living their values.* This suggests that their giving will shift toward charities they think of as spiritual and also that there may be an increase both in numbers of persons giving and in the level of their gifts.

• ABC can be especially attractive to younger adults. Busters (born between 1965 and 1977) are less concerned with acquiring possessions and more concerned with creating an extended family. Busters are pragmatic; they prefer *fixing* to *changing* the world. Busters insist on a hands-on knowledge of the organizations they support. ABC's programs meet their approval.

• ABC has credibility with audiences of diversity. Too many organizations wear blinders, seeing nonwhite and Hispanic individuals only as recipients of the organization's programs and services and failing to recognize the increasing interest among this growing segment of the population in supporting charities of their choice, and their increasing ability to do so. Affluent minorities are heavily civic; they look for stable organizations with traditional values.

• ABC is a good match with women, who have been shown to be more interested in supporting human service organizations than are men. This is good news for several reasons. There is a growing charitable independence among midlife women; they no longer automatically follow the philanthropic directions of fathers and spouses. In addition, women are

---

1. In the original report, a list of corporate examples was included here.

increasingly more affluent. And research confirms they are more charitable in general than are men.

Defining the Concerns

• Individuals in ABC's geographical area are not giving generously. According to the current Oregon Community Report *Giving in Oregon,*

> The percentage increase in average contributions by individuals in the United States was *twice* that of individuals in Oregon.

> The growth rate of average incomes was twice the growth rate of contributions.

> Individuals here give less than individuals in the neighboring states and less than individuals in other states with similar average incomes.

> Higher-income individuals are not giving at levels comparable to their counterparts from other states.

• The number of organizations seeking private support is increasing. There are approximately 5,000 not-for-profits in this community. Information gathered from United Way of Columbia Willamette for each county indicates literally hundreds of nonprofit private and government services available within the tricounty area. In terms of need, these services are complementary and in total do not meet the demonstrated needs in the area. For example, ABC's domestic violence shelter is one of five such shelters in the area. All are at full capacity most of the time, and all report turning away clients on a daily basis.

However, in fundraising, several of these shelters would be considered "competition" for ABC. Several other ABC services are also provided by other agencies and might be considered "competition." The list of competitors for private support is extensive.[2]

United Way has lost ground to inflation. As a result, it continues to cut back on funding allocations to many of its agencies. In turn, these organizations are becoming more assertive in asking the public directly for support. An interview with the president of the local United Way also indicated that that organization is moving toward funding pilot and innovative projects, rather than continuing operation support to its traditional partners, including ABC.

The effects of recent legislation are still being felt. Because of the severe cuts in state funding, some of the essential not-for-profits are in financial difficulties. More and more public agencies are entering the fundraising arena. Both the public school system and the public library now have

---

2. The original report included a list of some of the better-known competing organizations.

departments of development. As these institutions affect large numbers of citizens and their families directly, they must be viewed as strong competition for the charitable dollar.

Although the major capital campaigns at the "University of LMN" (goal: $140 million) and the "PQR Museum" (goal: $25 million) have been successfully completed, a number of campaigns are still currently underway. Several have set goals significantly higher than previously tried in this community. The original $30 million goal for "XYZ Hospital" has been expanded, and that organization expects to go back to several lead donors and ask these individuals, corporations, and foundations for extensions of pledges. As many of these lead donors are also prospective major donors to ABC, ABC might have difficulty getting large gifts from this group over the next one to three years.

Corporations are complaining about being "hit on." The companies interviewed for this report, including "FGH Bank" and "CDE Utilities"—both generous donors in the community—noted that they are receiving between fifty and sixty requests a week from charities.

• The ABC Organization—like most local not-for-profit organizations—is not "growing" its donors.

According to a recent article, local population is beginning to taper off, stabilizing at a growth rate of about 48,000 per year. Much of this continuing growth will not be in the metropolitan area.

As long as a population is growing, a broad-based acquisition strategy makes sense. However, once that population stabilizes, *after marketing* must become the priority. Although research has demonstrated the importance of renewal and upgrading, ABC does not have a strategy for encouraging renewal and upgrading among its donors. As most of the charities surveyed do not currently have such strategies, creating a renewal and upgrading strategy will provide ABC with an advantage.

Future acquisition should be selective. Generally, organizations here have done a good but not great job in getting new people involved as volunteers and in keeping committed persons involved. There is a window of opportunity for the ABC Organization to gain the commitment of large numbers of unaffiliated individuals. However, doing this will require a very different strategy and approach than has been used to acquire donors in the past. Although the population contains many diverse segments with different communication styles, ABC—like most of the state's not-for-profits—has used a homogeneous approach to donors.

> *ABC needs to segment its appeals to recognize that people from different generations, genders, and ethnic and racial backgrounds have different marketing keys and different money personalities.*

Conclusion: Although current giving here is disappointing, there are definite signs that significant increases are possible. Overall, the demographic and psychographic societal trends provide a window of opportunity for the ABC Organization to dramatically increase private support over the next five years.

Moving to the New Paradigm

Addressing Organizational Issues

Although the focus of this assessment is development, it is important to acknowledge that fundraising does not take place in a vacuum.

Consistently, those interviewed brought up concerns regarding communication, coordination, and trust throughout all levels of the organization. In addition, the ABC Organization has not reached out to show appreciation to its current supporters. And potential supporters have not been made welcome. This is an outgrowth of a *we-versus-them* mentality.

In the one-on-one and group interviews, ABC officers, staff, and volunteers made comments such as these:

"There is no accountability because key staff moves on."

"Extremely bottom-line oriented—regardless of the cost."

"Little information is recorded formally."

"Program areas don't communicate with development."

"Environment favors those who complain loudest."

"There's a flat organization chart yet a 'caste' system."

It should be recognized that the issues these comments reflect seriously affect an organization's ability to increase private support, and immediate action should be undertaken to address these issues at ABC.

Strengthening Board Leadership in Development

The ABC Organization's board of trustees has three fundraising roles:

1. Setting and approving development goals and objectives
2. Being an advocate for the organization and actively assisting in giving and getting
3. Exercising gift stewardship and accountability

Is ABC's board willing and able to focus on *giving and getting?* A number of board members were interviewed as part of the assessment process. They appear to be in agreement that the board has been moving toward a more active fundraising role but isn't there yet.

Among the comments offered by those board interviewees were these:

"We know we need to do more, but how?"

"We're more serious about our commitment now."

"We're ahead of the learning curve; need to make it work."

"We need fundraising training—we want it!"

As the organization positions itself for significant growth, the board must lead the way. The rationale for membership will be increasingly focused on each member's willingness and ability to provide financial support. *Leadership volunteers must give generously and must ask for money as their primary responsibilities.* The transition to these responsibilities can be painful.

Sustaining ABC's growth requires that its good friends take an objective look at their own willingness and ability to provide leadership in giving and getting. A key purpose of the development assessment is to provide current members of the board with the tools each one needs to personally address the question of his or her own role in the next phase of growth. A major goal of this personal assessment should be to center each member's focus on giving and getting.

Helping Board Members Understand Responsibilities

Board members need help in understanding their responsibilities, including giving and getting at leadership levels (see Questions for Board Members, which summarizes those responsibilities). The executive director, key officers, and program directors (furnishing the vision); the board (supplying the credibility); and the development staff (handling the logistics) must work together to identify, cultivate, and solicit the individuals, corporations and foundations from which private support is sought. *Every board member must be ready to play an active role in fundraising through his or her own financial support, through opening doors to giving by others, and through serving as an advocate for the ABC Organization.*

• Members of the board must be willing to serve as organizational spokespersons with donors and prospects. Among the activities not currently being done by ABC board members are these:

Helping to thank donors via phone calls and personalized notes

Hosting small groups of prospects

Actively networking in the greater community on a regular basis

Actively cultivating and soliciting an assigned group of prospects

---

ABC ORGANIZATION: QUESTIONS FOR BOARD MEMBERS

Each current and potential board member should be able to answer these questions about responsibilities affirmatively:

1. Do I understand the *plans* and *programs* for fundraising?

2. Do I fully understand and endorse the *case* why someone should contribute?

3. Do I myself *contribute* to the fullest measure within my means?

4. Do I continually offer additions to the *mailing list*?

5. Do I assist staff in *identifying* and *evaluating prospects*—individuals, corporations, and foundations?

6. Do I share in *cultivating* key prospects?

7. Do I make *introductions* so others can make a solicitation visit?

8. Do I *accompany* others in solicitation visits?

9. Do I write follow-up and acknowledgment *letters*?

10. Do I write *personal notes* on annual appeal letters?

11. Am I prepared to make a *solicitation* myself?

12. *Do I do what I say I will do?*

• Board members must understand the commitment they are making to the ABC Organization in agreeing to serve on its board. The nomination, recruitment, and orientation process must be formalized to enable potential and current board members to understand their fundraising responsibilities fully. Current board members have been recruited under "contracts" that haven't made their fundraising responsibilities clear. ABC must provide each current board member with the tools to feel confidence in her or his role.

1. A special board meeting should be set to help current board members evaluate their own roles and willingness to support the new paradigm fully.

2. A job description should be created that provides current (and potential) board members with a full explanation of the "contract" they are entering. A sample job description is provided in Resource A at the end of this report.

3. Each board member should receive a copy of the Better Business Bureau's *The Responsibilities of a Charity's Volunteer Board* (Publication No. 24–215) or a similar overview pamphlet.

• The board must set the pace for others. *Without 100 percent financial participation from the board it will be difficult to convince members of the broader community to join in the effort.* At the start of each fiscal year, board members must be helped to make a meaningful personal commitment. Obviously, the dollar amount will vary from one person to another; however, board members must make gifts that indicate true commitment. The board's own giving should kick off each fiscal year's fundraising: all board members should make or pledge their gifts prior to any solicitation in the general community.

The board members must be approached in a focused, coordinated way if they are to make (and complete) their pledges in a timely manner.

1. Each ongoing board member should be asked to recommit to the ABC Organization at the start of each fiscal year by signing his or her name to the mission or board job description. A token gift of $1—signed by the board member—should be sought from each member to symbolically demonstrate 100 percent participation. (These activities should be part of the yearly board retreat, which will also cover the board annual giving campaign and fundraising responsibilities.)

2. Any board members who have not made a gift or pledge for the current fiscal year by this time must be visited immediately by the board president. The goal for the board is always 100 percent participation at a meaningful level.

3. For the upcoming fiscal year and each year following, the board campaign should begin all annual fundraising efforts. It should be scheduled for August and September—two months before the start of ABC's fiscal year (October through September)—and be completed by the first board meeting of the new year (the third Thursday in October). A committee consisting of the current board president, past board president, and Development Committee chair should be responsible for the campaign.

• The members of the board must have a support system in order to raise money. Most volunteers (and many staff) perceive fundraising as adversarial. Unless they are helped to understand their role as advocates and facilitators, they will be understandably reluctant to participate.

1. A key development staff member, such as the vice president of development, must have responsibility for working with board members one-on-one to track the progress of their fundraising assignments. It is his or her responsibility to keep the executive director and board president fully informed of any concerns.

2. Fundraising training should be scheduled regularly and should include opportunities for role-playing and the raising of concerns. Few individuals *like* to raise money. This discomfort needs to be addressed if volunteers and staff are to be effective.

• Leadership volunteers must be recruited who will ask for money as their primary responsibility. Discussions with board members reveal that many board members are already giving to capacity and do not have the contacts or ability to raise large dollars. There is a need to attract board members with broad *name recognition* who are willing to give and get. Staff must work with current board members to identify, cultivate, and involve these potential board members with ABC. To formalize this recruitment process, ABC must take these steps:

1. The board's Trusteeship Committee should function year-round. Potential board members should be regularly reviewed, interviewed, and assessed. Ideally, they will have served in some other volunteer capacity or have made gifts at a significant level prior to being asked to serve.

2. The performance of new board members should be evaluated over a year's probationary period. Each new member should be provided with a board mentor, and there should be a "contract" between mentor and volunteer that specifies how they will work together. The Trusteeship Committee should meet quarterly to assess performance.

3. The board should become more diversified ethnically, so that the volunteer leadership reflects the diversity of the population ABC serves. This requires a proactive commitment to recruitment of persons of color and women. ABC should identify vehicles such as alternative media to communicate with and widen its pool of potential members.

Setting and Approving Development Goals and Objectives

The ABC Organization needs a full ten-year strategic plan so it can set specific fundraising goals. Although it is obvious that current fundraising is below potential, vague growth objectives will not provide the impetus for energizing development efforts. (This has been addressed in other sections of this report.)

In addition, ABC needs to revitalize the board's Development Committee. Under the leadership of the chief fundraising executive, this committee's role is to guide the fundraising process. The principal role of the Development Committee is to institutionalize fund development within the board itself. The accompanying list shows suggested specific responsibilities for the Development Committee.

ABC ORGANIZATION: RESPONSIBILITIES FOR THE DEVELOPMENT COMMITTEE

1. Providing leadership for the organization's fund development efforts.

2. Encouraging a sense of ownership about fund development among fellow board members.

3. Working with staff and the board finance committee to analyze the organization's financial needs and determine realistic gift revenue goals for the budget.

4. Assisting staff in the design of an annual fund development plan and presenting the plan to the board.

5. With the assistance of the full board and staff, identifying and cultivating prospects and determining their readiness to give and gift potential.

6. With the assistance of the full board and staff, identifying, recruiting, and training development volunteers and monitoring volunteer performance.

7. Assisting staff in the design of a donor recognition program.

8. Helping staff monitor the progress and effectiveness of fundraising efforts and make necessary changes.

9. Working with staff to identify and resolve strategic issues that affect ABC's ability to raise funds.

10. Making recommendations to the board about fund development policy.

Developing Gift Stewardship and Accountability Guidelines

Gift stewardship and accountability guidelines need to be formulated before the development strategy is implemented.

Donors are insisting on better accountability and stewardship from not-for-profits. Before an organization can go out and raise money, it must establish what gifts are acceptable and how it will handle gifts received. The ABC Organization owes that to potential contributors and to the board: accountability and stewardship are overwhelming concerns of today's donors.

Although ABC has the beginnings of gift stewardship and accountability guidelines, they are not complete. ABC needs to review how it will handle specific gift situations that may arise, recover fundraising costs, and provide donor recognition to donors and key volunteers. Among the questions that need to be addressed are these:

Who can accept gifts? Does the vice president of development have that right? Does the board president have that right? Does gift acceptance require a full board or board committee meeting? Gift acceptance policies will protect the organization. Too often, a well-meaning volunteer doesn't check before telling the donor that his or her gift will be welcome, but sometimes gifts have complications. A policy that requires review by a committee provides a cooling-off period.

What types of gifts will ABC accept? There may be a limit to what ABC wants to handle in terms of management and stewardship. ABC may not want any gifts of real estate or may want to accept gifts of stock, real estate, and real property only with the condition that such gifts can be put up for sale immediately. Each organization must balance out its ability to manage long-term assets with the potential donor's needs.

How will ABC show its appreciation? Recognition needs to be consistent for all donors of similar gifts. ABC needs to decide minimum gift levels for namings, endowments, and other types of fundraising. Will donors receive plaques or premiums? There's a cost involved. How much is to be given back?

At what level may donors restrict their gifts? The further up the gift-giving ladder, the higher the proportion of restricted gifts. Very few donors of $1 million allow an organization to use their gift in any way the charity chooses. At what level—if any—will ABC allow the donor to direct the use of the gift?

How will ABC recover operating and fundraising costs from unrestricted, restricted, and endowment gifts? There are numerous methods for recovering fundraising costs, ranging from levying a percentage tax on all restricted gifts to using unrestricted gifts to cover costs on restricted fundraising. Once ABC decides on its policy, volunteers and staff must communicate this information to potential donors.

What levels of funding are required for endowments, facility and room namings, and life income vehicles including trusts, annuities, and pooled income funds? The levels of funding required need to be consistent for all donors: ABC can't "sell" a room to a member of the board for less than that same type of room is "sold" to the general public. And it's important not to accept less than is needed to handle the costs involved with an endowment's payout. It's better for everyone if the rules are set out clearly, in advance.

How will ABC handle the possibility of immediate costs associated with a long-term gift? For example, when a donor gives a gift of stock worth $100,000, the Financial Committee may wish to retain the stock for a time, believing the value will increase substantially over the next few years, but the donor may specify that the gift fund a program to the amount of $2,000 per year and may request that payouts begin in the current fiscal year. How will ABC handle this?

How will ABC internally value in-kind donations? Although the IRS does not allow not-for-profits to valuate in-kind gifts, ABC may want to provide some kind of recognition that does not indicate a specific tax value.

Once ABC has formulated the initial answers to these questions, it should create a document titled "Gift Stewardship Guidelines and Policies." This document will need to be reviewed on a yearly basis. Sample guidelines are provided in Resource B.

Determining the Fundraising Role of the Executive Director

Although the board provides the community's "seal of approval" for ABC and the director of development is responsible for carrying out the logistics of the development program and fundraising methodologies, *it is the role of the executive director to articulate the organization's vision.*

- The executive director needs to make the time to network within the greater community on a regular basis.

   1. The executive director should identify all available civic and community organizations, such as Rotary, Lions, Chamber of Commerce, and so forth, and decide which meetings he should attend regularly and which ones from time to time. The executive director should choose at least one community organization to make a commitment to and volunteer for.

   2. ABC should have a brochure or letter made up and sent to organizations indicating the availability of ABC's executive director (and other staff and volunteer leadership) to speak before professional groups. Actively seek at least one such opportunity every other month.

   3. ABC should inform the media that its executive director is available when they need a resource to provide background information on subjects within ABC's areas of expertise.

- The executive director must serve as the *voice and face* of ABC with donors and prospects.

   1. Each week, a list of donors making gifts of over $500 should be given to the executive director by the vice president of development. The executive director must put aside the necessary time to make a phone call of appreciation to each of these $500+ donors *within forty-eight hours* of receiving this list. The purpose of the call is not to ask for more money but to demonstrate ABC's appreciation to the donor. Effective thank-you calls use these steps:

   Thank the donor

   Ask why she or he supports ABC

   Add to the donor's information if appropriate

   Offer to visit or send information

   Thank the donor again

2. The executive director should put aside at least one block of time monthly (best blocked out on a regular basis, for example, the last Friday afternoon of each month) to be scheduled by the vice president of development. The vice president should develop a list of board members, donors and past donors, and prospects to be invited to visit with the executive director at a mutually convenient location to get better acquainted. Although individual appointments are best, breakfast or luncheon meetings of small groups are also recommended. The office of the executive director, rather than the board room, should be used to maintain informality.

• The executive director must provide the Development Office with the necessary backup and support.

1. Currently, lines of reporting and accountability are not clear to staff or to volunteers. The executive director should address these issues.

2. The executive director should attend yearly one fundraising conference with the vice president of development. The Council for Advancement and Support of Education (CASE) offers several workshops for leadership in development that might be appropriate to explore.

3. The executive director must support appropriate growth in the Development Office budget and staffing. Interviews with development staff indicate that both professional and support staff feel unappreciated. Average raises are low; resources are often minimal; staff work long hours. Although correction of all the concerns may take time, an important starting point will be the articulation by the executive director that he concurs that the work of the Development Office is important.

4. ABC should integrate development into management, program, and board functions and keep lines of communication open among them. The vice president of development is not automatically invited to many organizational meetings. This officer must be considered part of ABC's leadership team.

Reorganizing the Development Office

The ABC Organization must reorganize its development and public relations functions. To reach the desired financial goals requires a more coordinated approach than has been the case. Public relations, publications, grants, and fundraising should all be housed in the Office of Development. A centralized approach would allow ABC to integrate all outreach functions.

Currently, reporting relations are confused. As a result, there is a lack of accountability. The current organizational structure results in important development steps falling through the cracks, duplication of activities, and a lack of synergy. The centralized approach will recognize that although key ABC officers and program directors should be involved in major gifts cultivation, smaller gift acquisition and the acknowledgment and after-marketing functions are best handled by professionals. Centralizing will result in economies of scale as well.

• The position of vice president of development should be redefined to oversee all areas of outreach including planning, interpretation, coordination, implementation, and management of all fundraising activities.

1. Serving as the chief development officer, she or he advises and makes recommendations to the ABC executive director regarding overall department and organizational goals, objectives, programs, procedures, and policies wherever fundraising and other appropriate activities are involved and serves as the key development staff liaison to the board.

2. The vice president of development's job description should be redone to include the responsibilities outlined in the accompanying list.

ABC ORGANIZATION: RESPONSIBILITIES FOR VICE PRESIDENT OF DEVELOPMENT

1. Provide leadership for the organization's fund development and friend raising efforts.

2. Work with program directors and the board finance committee to analyze the organization's financial needs and determine realistic gift revenue goals.

3. Work with key ABC leadership to identify and resolve strategic issues that affect the ability to raise funds.

4. With the assistance of the board, cultivate and solicit the highest level of prospects.

5. With the assistance of the board and staff, identify, recruit, and train volunteers and monitor volunteer performance.

6. Know all donors of $1,000 or more, who they work with on the staff and board, and the plan for stewarding them.

7. Oversee staff and volunteer visits to major donors and prospects.

8. Direct development staff in the design of an annual fund development plan.

9. Help staff monitor progress and effectiveness of fundraising efforts and make necessary changes.

10. Make recommendations to the executive director and board regarding fund development policy.

11. Create an atmosphere of collegiality.

• There are gaps between current Development Office job descriptions and job responsibilities. Many of the development staff noted that their day-to-day responsibilities bear little resemblance to the job descriptions under which they were hired. A key complaint among staff is that responsibilities are added without any attempt to remove other jobs, creating a frustrating sense of constantly being under pressure to outperform.

The reporting structure within the Office of Development should be reorganized for better performance and accountability. Currently, the reporting relationship is confused with various development staff reporting to individuals in other departments.

1. Under the leadership of a vice president of development, the organizational chart should be redrawn and the current professional positions should be revamped as shown in the Proposed Organizational Chart, which suggests the overall areas of job responsibility for each position.

2. In order to ascertain whether (a) current staff are using their time wisely, (b) current staff are competent, and (c) additional staff are necessary, a time log of actual work should be kept for each person. Then job descriptions should be revised accordingly.

3. Over time, additional professional positions need to be added. Given the potential for major and planned giving, ABC should expect to add two more directors in the next two years. In addition, associate director positions—handling prospect research and the middle tier of donors ($100 to $999) should be considered (see the Proposed Organizational Chart).

4. Support positions appear adequate at this time but should be carefully monitored. Donors judge organizations on their customer service. The customer service concerns at ABC do not appear to be a result of understaffing but rather of the need to redefine jobs and monitor performance.

• In order to create a positive working environment, staff turnover must be kept to a minimum. This means that to find (and keep) qualified development officers, ABC must be willing to reevaluate its levels of compensation. There is a significant gap between salaries being offered at competitive not-for-profits and at ABC.

According to a recent nationwide study, top development officers at health and human services organizations comparable to the ABC Organization in size, needs, and fundraising responsibilities received an average salary of almost $145,000 in 1995, an increase of 6 percent over 1994. Compensation ranged from a low of $45,000 to a high of $257,200. Benefits typically included professional dues, travel reimbursement, health insurance, disability insurance, and car mileage. Performance bonuses are becoming frequent as well. Because the competition for qualified development professionals is increasing locally as elsewhere, salary and benefit packages should be reviewed to be sure they are consistent with those offered by the competition and, preferably, fall at the upper end of competing offers.

Given competitive salaries in the local fundraising community, ABC should be prepared to pay $65,000 to $75,000+ for its senior development officer. The current compensation at ABC is $50,000. Specialized development officers (directors of major giving, planned giving, corporate and foundation relations, and public relations) are receiving $35,000 to $55,000 elsewhere in the local fundraising community. ABC is paying $26,000 to $40,000.

ABC ORGANIZATION: PROPOSED ORGANIZATIONAL CHART

VICE PRESIDENT OF DEVELOPMENT

- Oversees Office of Development and community relations
- Supervises all staff
- Acts as board liaison
- Is responsible for major and planned gifts over $100,000

DIRECTORS OF DEVELOPMENT

Annual Giving
- Gift acknowledgment
- General acquisition through direct mail
- Donor renewal and upgrading strategies

Major Giving
- Cultivation and solicitation of $1,000+ donors and prospects

Planned Giving
- Cultivation and solicitation of bequests, gifts other than cash, and life income arrangements.

Corporate and Foundation Relations
- Grant writing
- Research
- Tracking
- Sponsorship

DIRECTOR OF PUBLIC RELATIONS AND OUTREACH

- Media relations
- Speakers Bureau
- Special events strategy
- Publications and newsletters
- Volunteers:
  - Recruitment
  - Training
  - Recognition

ASSOCIATE DIRECTORS (2)
not currently funded

- Prospect research
- Leadership Giving Program ($100–$999)

ADMINISTRATIVE ASSISTANTS (2–3)

- Screen calls
- Scheduling and coordination
- Clerical duties

GIFT PROCESSING ASSISTANTS (4)

- Data entry
- Gift acknowledgment
- Bulk mail assistance
- Clerical backup

- A strong support system for development staff must be created. ABC has a significant number of development professionals—it must invest in them. Continuing fundraising education must be a priority.

1. High-quality training should be offered on a regular schedule.

2. There are core competencies that all development staff should be educated in along with specialty training. ABC offers training in computer programs on a regular basis, for example.

3. All development staff should belong to and attend meetings of the local professional fundraising societies—the local chapter of the National Society of Fund Raising Executives and the Willamette Valley Development Officers. There are also specialty organizations, such as the Planned Giving Roundtable, that are useful. Currently, attendance at such meetings is spotty.

4. There is no separate budget line for professional development. Monies should be put in the development budget for development staff to attend local, regional, and national conferences offered by organizations such as the National Society of Fund Raising Executives, the Portland State University Center on Philanthropy, and so forth. Policies should be implemented that answer questions about how often staff may go to out-of-town conferences, what is expected as a result, and similar concerns.

Computerizing

The heart of a strong development program lies in its ability to identify, track, and respond personally to its prospects. As the ABC Organization has just put in place a new, computerized development system, it is difficult to make a realistic judgment about how well that system will serve ABC's needs, so at this time, the assessment will not make recommendations on the development system. There are three key areas of concern that need to be assessed on an ongoing basis and with the help of both development staff and management information system (MIS) staff:

- The development system must provide sophisticated information to staff. The ABC Organization must be able to segment its database both demographically and psychographically. Both acquisition and after marketing must use the technology and communication vehicles preferred by various segments of the population. Mass marketing will no longer produce the results the ABC Organization seeks.

- There should be minimum dependence on MIS. All development staff must be fully trained and able to use the system for acknowledging gifts, inputting data, and producing standard reports. The development system must be easy to use.

- The system should be able to handle prospect management functions. Staff must be able to

> Look at affiliations at a glance
>
> Process queries and sorts
>
> Receive prompts for flagging and use a comments field

Making the Budget Commitment

The reorganization of the development operations will require a significant commitment of resources: the ABC Organization should be willing and able to commit to a three-year start-up investment. Staff and key volunteers must understand that results will not be immediately forthcoming and that without a continuing commitment to development the program should not be undertaken.

The budget for the Development Office must demonstrate a commitment to increased costs as an anticipated result of moving to the new paradigm. Many of these expenses will be one-time costs. Expense areas that must be included in the budget are these:

> Staffing positions, including benefits
>
> Consulting positions
>
> Office overhead
>
> Donor relations and gift stewardship
>
> Gift acknowledgment and appreciation
>
> Prospect research
>
> Publications, including newsletters, brochures, envelopes
>
> Computer support and upgrades
>
> Staff training, including professional memberships and publications
>
> Board meetings
>
> Board training
>
> Direct fundraising
>
>> Major gifts
>>
>> Planned gifts
>>
>> Annual gifts
>>
>> Special events
>>
>> Corporate and foundation relations

Although the staff of the Office of Development have produced significant income for ABC each year, their raises have been limited to 3 percent annually. ABC's leadership must be helped to understand the work done by fundraisers and agree to reward staff for extraordinary efforts.

Most organizations underestimate the investment required to *seed* a development effort. The total cost of fundraising is considerably higher than the public and organizations understand. This cost needs to be viewed as an investment. Carefully thought out performance and evaluation steps are required. This is discussed in depth in the next section.

A tentative budget is shown here (Office of Development Budget Summary), based on the recommended development strategy. Once the strategy outlined in this development assessment is approved, development staff will refine the strategy and the budget.

ABC ORGANIZATION: OFFICE OF DEVELOPMENT BUDGET SUMMARY, FISCAL 199_

		Income	Expense
DIRECT	Annual giving (gifts to $249)	$3,185,000	$589,000
	Major giving and planned giving (gifts of $250+)	$1,825,000 outright gifts $3,300,000 planned gifts and pledges	$130,000
	Corporate and foundation relations	$250,000 grant writing $356,772 United Way allocations $82,000 United Way donor-designated gifts $10,000 Federal Combined Campaign	$6,500
	Public relations and outreach	$180,000 cash donations $750,000 in-kind donations	$105,100
INDIRECT	Overall Office of Development		$698,778 salaries $15,000 professional development $35,000 occupancy $10,000 office equipment and furnishings $15,000 telephone $10,000 general office supplies $25,000 computer and printer equipment
TOTALS		$5,888,772 outright cash gifts $3,300,000 pledges and planned gifts $750,000 in-kind donations	$1,644,378
GRAND TOTAL		$9,938,772	$1,644,378

Evaluating Current and Future Fundraising Methodologies

The ABC Organization has never tracked its development costs fully. The CBBB (Charitable Better Business Bureau) and NCIB (National Charities Information Board), in their "bottom-line" guidelines, allow fundraising costs to be equivalent to 35 percent and 40 percent, respectively, of funds allocated for programs and services and administration and management. It is not unusual during the start-up phase of a development program for costs to be 50 percent (or greater) of revenues raised. Start-up can take up to three years. Once a program is in its maturity, fundraising costs tend to drop to 20 to 30 percent overall. ABC's current development strategy has been in place for upward of ten years.

ABC's latest annual report gives these expense ratios for fundraising:

Current cash gifts alone	28 percent
With in-kind gifts added	25 percent
With pledges and planned gifts added	16.5 percent

However, in reviewing the costs of fundraising, it was determined that ABC has reported extremely low fundraising costs because many of the indirect costs of development—salaries and office costs—were not considered.

When these indirect costs are added in, the revised costs are as follows:

Current cash gifts alone	58 percent
With in-kind gifts added	35 percent
With pledges and planned gifts added	26.5 percent

In addition, different fundraising methodologies have different costs attached, with major individual gift fundraising being the most cost efficient and direct mail and special events being the least cost efficient. Again, ABC's costs have been obscured:

**Direct Costs
(Fundraising *Without* Office of Development Costs)**

Annual giving	18 percent
Major and planned giving	12 percent
Corporate and foundation relations	1 percent
Special events	30 percent

**Direct and Indirect Costs
(Fundraising *with* Office of Development Costs)**

Annual giving	36 percent
Major and planned giving	16 percent
Corporate and foundation relations	39 percent
Special events	63 percent

The revised numbers demonstrate that for ABC's mature development program, only the fundraising cost for major and planned giving is well within accepted limits.

Evaluation of fundraising should not be limited to cost to income ratios. The effectiveness of major and planned giving should be measured by the development of meaningful relations with donors and prospects as well. Short-term fundraising results are not the best evaluation measures, rather contacts and activity level are.

Once a commitment to the proposed strategy and its recommendations is made, the ABC Organization should review the specific goals and objectives for each of its fundraising strategies, looking at what is possible rather than at historical precedents. Linking strategy to results, accountabilities can be set for each area of fundraising. Measurable steps for evaluating achievement need to be developed, including fundraising objectives, goals, and a timeline for implementation. Measurement of overall fundraising and of each fundraising program is necessary for evaluation of how effective the development strategy has been.

Evaluating Fundraising Staff

Staff evaluations need to be better linked to performance. The current evaluation structure is not useful in linking budget goals and objectives back to the staff person (or persons) having accountability for the results. Working with the Personnel Department, the vice president of development should revise the current evaluation forms.

The Proposed Development Strategy

The following section focuses on recommended specific steps to be taken once the issues addressed previously under organizational issues, board leadership, and reorganizing the development office are addressed.

Moving from a Broad-Based to a Focused Development Strategy

The ABC Organization has been reactive in its approach to fundraising, relying on a broad-based, undifferentiated development strategy. ABC cannot reach new levels of private support unless it determines which fundraising methodologies will provide the greatest successes in the years ahead. It doesn't matter what the past successes have been: when the paradigm shifts, everyone starts over. Unless ABC carefully chooses its development priorities, it will go in too many directions and put too much time into fundraising programs that bring in only a fraction of the potential possible.

ABC has not defined its *best* donors. The components of ABC's development strategy must be rethought and reordered, and ABC must prioritize its various audiences, putting its efforts where the best results are likely. Each audience segment needs to be addressed uniquely. The goal is to go deep, rather than wide, within each segment. ABC should prioritize its donors and prospects according to

Their level of interest in the mission

Their ability to make larger versus smaller gifts

In order for a not-for-profit to keep growing, it must have a prospect and donor base that fulfills three stages of giving (these stages are defined further in the accompanying table, Three Stages of Giving):

1. A group of prospects who care—*acquisition*

2. A group of repeat donors who care deeply—*renewal*

3. A group of major donors who care deeply enough—*upgrading*

High-interest donors. The most time and energy should be spent with those audiences already highly involved with the ABC Organization. *Strategy:* create *core donors* through frequency, upgrading, and expansion of giving.

THREE STAGES OF GIVING

UPGRADE Those Who Care Deeply Enough to Make Major and Planned Gifts (High Interest)	RENEW Those Who Care Deeply Enough to Become Annual Donors (Medium Interest)	ACQUIRE Those Who Care Enough to Make First Gifts (Low Interest)
Expectancy notifications	Annual donors (2 gifts or more in 18 months)	First-time donors of modest amounts (under $25)
Board members	Lapsed donors (24–36 months)	Targeted audiences for acquisition (affluent)
Donors for 5, 10, 15 Years	First-time donors of $26–$99	Events audiences for acquisition (modest)
One-time gifts above $100	Repeat memorial and tribute donors	Bought or traded lists: external audiences for acquisition (very modest)
Internal short list of donors of wealth identified through research		First-time memorial and tribute donors (modest)
External short list of prospects of wealth identified through research		Friends and family members of current donors

Medium-interest donors and prospects. Next, ABC should focus on keeping the donors it has. *Strategy:* increase renewal rates, reconnect lapsed donors, and work with affluent, self-identifying prospects.

Low-interest donors and prospects. Finally, ABC should work to keep its support base expanding. *Strategy:* encourage modest donors to upgrade, and selectively acquire new donors, with an emphasis on more affluent prospects. Spend a very modest amount of time, effort, and resources on low-level acquisition via identified internal and external vehicles.

Increasing Community Understanding of ABC

To reach new supporters will require more education and communication. The ABC Organization needs to do a better job in articulating its case for support.

- There are four major strategic goals for the Public Relations Office:

  1. *Crisis management:* to ensure that unfavorable publicity regarding ABC is prevented or minimized in a timely fashion

  2. *Public information:* to ensure that the public receives information on ABC's programs and services in a positive, timely fashion

  3. *Leadership giving and volunteerism:* to ensure that persons of *influence and affluence* in the community see ABC as their organization of choice

  4. *General fundraising awareness:* to ensure that the general public chooses ABC as one of their charities and to encourage selected segments to give more than fair share gifts

By making the position of director of public relations and outreach responsible for media relations, a speakers bureau, special events strategies for friend raising, volunteer activities, and publications and newsletters, ABC will have more control over the look of its communications pieces and will create a *synergy* between the various areas of outreach and of building ABC's image (see Public Relations and Outreach Strategy).

- Immediately, a number of items should be addressed by the director of public relations and outreach, including the following:

  1. A full plan should be designed for improving ABC's image, addressing outreach via media relations, a speakers bureau, and events. Also a unique selling proposition (USP) and identity for all written materials needs to be created.

  2. Focus groups should be held regularly that enable ABC to involve key influential and affluent persons in the community in outreach. This will enable the organization to grow a better pool of key volunteers and donors.

3. Cultivation materials need to be developed that discuss all aspects of ABC's outreach. Especially urgent are these:

> *A video that tells the ABC story:* The ABC Organization already has such a vehicle; however, it appears dated. The new video should be tested with persons *outside* the ABC family to see how effective it is.

> *An overall brochure:* There is almost too much printed material available on ABC. Prospects and donors need to be able to turn to one piece for an overview.

> *A quarterly newsletter:* The donor newsletter needs to come out on a regular schedule of four times a year. Again, ABC should get feedback from outsiders to see if this vehicle is meeting its goal of enabling prospects to get better acquainted with ABC. A newsletter—even one with a gift reply envelope—is not viewed by many prospects as an appeal for money. They are more willing to open and read such materials than other fundraising mailings.

4. More personal and more visual fundraising materials need to be developed. These include a general fundraising brochure that emphasizes giving at $100 and above, a business partners brochure, a bequest and planned giving brochure that emphasizes case examples, a memorial and tribute giving brochure featuring namings and restricted gifts for various program centers, more involving and segmented acknowledgment letters, and consistent reply vehicles.

Increasing Results by Strengthening the Individual Fundraising Components

Major Giving

ABC has not successfully managed its major gift program nor put emphasis on the major gift process. Although the numbers of people who have been contacted by the Major Gifts Department are impressive, the results are not. There appear to be two overall concerns:

ABC has not articulated that it needs major gifts.

ABC has not identified those who can make such gifts.

The main problem seems to be that unconsciously perhaps, the ABC Organization is sending its donors a signal that significant giving is not needed from supporters. This is largely a result of not having articulated the funds needed by ABC both short term and long term. There is no sense of urgency attached to the ask. ABC has not challenged donors to give more. It must create a sense of urgency, enabling itself to challenge current and new donors to reach toward higher levels of partnership.

ABC ORGANIZATION: PUBLIC RELATIONS AND OUTREACH STRATEGY, FISCAL YEAR 1998

	Strategy	Staff Responsible	Income Goals	Expenses
Donor relations and stewardship events Event name and date	Let various departments run events, with input from PR for community awareness and media	JD	$?? in-kind (cash donations shown under major, annual, corporate, and foundation giving)	$10,000
Public relations Crisis management Public information Leadership giving General fundraising awareness	Develop internal and external plan Stories, articles Video and donor circles Business journal ads Paid ads	JD	— — (Under major giving) (Under major giving) (Under annual giving)	($40,000 costs shown under staffing) $20,000 $17,000 (7 ads) $10,000
Volunteers	Recruitment and training Coordination and tracking Recognition	JD	— — —	$500 $500 $2,500 (event and certificates)
Speakers bureau	United Way Clubs and service organizations Other	JD	(Under corporate and foundation giving)	$2,500
Media relations	Public service announcements Clipping service	JD	—	$2,000
Marketing	Camp facilities (for FY 1999) Christmas ornaments	JD	$10,600 ($2,500 in-kind donation)	$600 (mailing and promotion) (2,500 ornaments)
Fundraising events	Dinner dance Community luncheon Golf tournament		$27,500 $130,000 ($50,000 sponsorships) ($80,000 tables) $12,000	$5,000 $25,000 $10,000
Budget totals			$180,000	$105,100

The ABC Organization will celebrate its 120th anniversary in 2003. This milestone offers a unique opportunity. Raising awareness of the ABC Organization movement and its 120-year tradition of leadership is a necessary lead-in to any increased fundraising.

The comprehensive 120th Anniversary Campaign should have three distinct thrusts:

1. *Outreach/educational component*: to help the broader community understand what the ABC Organization is and what it contributes to the community. This could include public speaking, public service announcements, a brochure of hints and tips for individuals and businesses, and so forth.

2. *Recognition component*: to find opportunities to publicly thank those who support, guide, and use ABC's efforts. This could include expanded volunteer, staff, and donor appreciation events.

3. *Fundraising component*: mainly to increase major and planned giving to create the organization's endowment but also to develop opportunities for increased annual giving.

An anniversary campaign is a major undertaking. It is important to begin the planning and preliminary stages of this campaign now. The next year will be needed to formalize the campaign objectives and format, identifying campaign leadership and volunteers and beginning the initial (quiet) phase of leadership pledges before going public.

In addition, the Office of Development has not managed the major gift process. Not enough is known about the current donor base outside of its recorded gift history. (And even this is open to question because, according to the development director, donation histories prior to 1991 were not recorded.) Donors and prospects must be carefully tracked. It is necessary to have regular quarterly meetings of the development director and staff to review the status of each major donor, and internal meetings to coordinate prospect visits.

• The Major and Planned Giving Departments must create a program of ongoing prospect research to prioritize donors and prospects with both the resources and interest to make major gifts and to create a strategy that involves the board and key ABC officers in the cultivation and solicitation of major gift prospects.

1. The Development Office needs to create a donor survey. This is the single best vehicle for collecting usable demographic and psychographic information. It should be sent as part of a welcoming packet to all donors, and it must be designed so the information gathered can be added to the computerized database.

2. The Development Office has attempted to research prospects, but there may be much greater potential in the current donor base than is realized at this time. A solid program of prospect research needs to be instituted at once. Administrative assistants in the Major and Planned Giving Departments should be given the task of collecting local not-for-profit honor rolls and checking to see if $500+ donors to agencies similar to ABC are on ABC's database.

3. Each week the social pages, newsmaker pages, and so forth from local newspapers should be collected. The administrative assistants can check whether names in these sections appear on ABC's database.

4. A screening and overlay package (a purchased service that examines an organization's donors against database indicators of wealth, including stock and real estate holdings) should be decided upon for purchase and use in conjunction with the 120th Anniversary Campaign.

• Work to move donors up the donor pyramid by cultivating current and past donors capable of giving annually at the $100+ level. To do this requires that ABC (a) educate donors about how giving more makes a difference and (b) provide donors with incentives for moving from one level to another. (Note: donors of $100 to $249 will be handled primarily through direct-mail and telephone contact. The Major and Planned Giving Departments must coordinate closely with the Annual Giving Department on this activity.)

1. A Leadership Giving Recognition Program should be created to serve as a framework. This program should be a reward and acknowledgment to donors that choose the ABC Organization as a giving priority. It should also serve as a marketing tool, encouraging prospects to consider committing at the $100+ level with their first gifts.

The Leadership Giving Recognition Program should encompass all the following levels of giving:

Planned gifts: The program acknowledges all amounts, future and past.

Cumulative giving: The program acknowledges total giving of $5,000 or more.

Annual giving: The program acknowledges yearly (total) giving of $100 or more.

2. ABC should create an identity for its Leadership Giving Recognition Program, using the following elements:

A general brochure to explain the concept. A shorter version that will be used to confirm membership is also needed. Both versions will be used as part of the after-marketing matrix.

A distinctive letterhead.

A certificate of appreciation for participants.

A quarterly special report or newsletter for members.

An annual thank you event.

Invitations to informational and stewardship events.

- It takes as long as thirty-four months to educate, cultivate, and bring to satisfactory solicitation a truly major gifts prospect. For ABC, based on past giving histories, that major gift begins at $5,000. The ABC Organization needs to begin the cultivation process now with those who can already be identified as having major gift potential and who are already signaling interest. By aiming to continually increase involvement and by launching its 120th Anniversary Campaign, ABC will be in a good position to encourage truly major giving from these individuals.

1. The Development Office should finalize the funding priorities and launch the initial quiet phase of the campaign by focusing on gifts from the board in the following ways:

Holding a retreat to introduce the vision and explain the costs associated with that vision

Having the vice president of development, in conjunction with the officers of the board, visit with each board member individually to discuss commitments

2. The Development Office should develop a short list of major gift prospects and begin an ongoing series of individual and group visits with these prospects, involving the members of the board and key ABC officers. Small dinner parties, for example, can be hosted by board members.

- Create special programs that encourage buy-in at the $250 to $4,999 level. Use the concept of *community investors*, for example, encouraging the purchase of multiple shares of "stock" priced at $250 a share. Each "shareholder" becomes an investor in a restricted fund. Quarterly, shareholders will receive a special report detailing how one-half of the fund's earnings will be used by ABC for areas of greatest need and presenting recommended programs (up to four) for funding. Shareholders may attend quarterly meetings to hear informational presentations and "vote" or may elect to send back "proxies."

1. The Development Office should create a committee to identify the concept to be used. It should deliver materials (use a video).

2. It should begin to identify prospects by holding a quarterly review of contacts made with major gift donors.

Target current donors ($100 to $249) for upgrading.

Identify high-potential donors (use prospect research and external screening to identify donors who are currently not giving at a level above $99 but who could move up rapidly if motivated).

Compile or acquire a test acquisition list of highly affluent prospects.

- ABC should use direct mail and telephone to create specialized appeals that will attract $100 to $249 donors. (This is discussed later under annual giving.)

Planned Giving

It is suggested that ABC consider merging the Planned Giving and Major Giving Departments, as many of the same donors and prospects are common to both. This will enable ABC to more effectively make use of limited staff resources and provide donors and prospects with one professional staff contact person instead of (often) two.

ABC's planned giving program is well-organized. The strategy is sound and progress is being made. The Planned Giving Department has identified a logical base of supporters of approximately 3,500 individuals. Appropriate vehicles—coupons, ads, and so forth—are in place to identify interest. A successful planned giving program builds on a foundation of interest and understanding among potential and existing constituencies so that an appeal for bequests and other planned gifts follows logically from ongoing communications. Committed donors like the idea that their generosity continues forever.

Although conventional thinking suggests it will take three to five years before an organization sees solid (that is, dollar) returns from a planned giving program, it is clear that the momentum is present in the current program.

- ABC needs to improve the organization of its planned giving program. To succeed with a planned giving program requires a long-term commitment. Not only must an organization accept that there is increasing competition from other not-for-profits for ultimate gifts, but it must recognize that planned gifts are solicited in the present for the future. If the organization changes, is perceived differently, enters into a crisis, uses different staff and volunteers, and so on, the gift may be withdrawn or redefined. Planned giving programs also require financial resources. The thrust of such programs is informational and educational. They require a constant flow of brochures, flyers, inserts, newsletters, workshops, and visits. A successful planned giving program is the result of carefully coordinating ongoing vehicles to provide information, cultivation, and—finally—solicitation. These three components do not necessarily exist linearly; rather, they overlap and must be done continuously.

There needs to be strong coordination between the major and planned giving strategies. ABC should use planned gifts to open the way to a greater number of major current gifts. The best source of major endowment gifts is often a planned gift such as a bequest.

Finally, ABC's guidelines determining acceptance and stewardship policies for planned gifts are incomplete. This should be addressed when the general gift acceptance and stewardship guidelines are made more complete, as recommended elsewhere.

- ABC's marketing effort for planned gifts should be expanded.

1. The Development Office should continue to cultivate the traditional audiences using advertisements and direct mail.

2. While continuing the cultivation strategy that has worked well for ABC, the Development Office should carefully look for a few nontraditional audiences or ways of expanding. Suggested strategies include the following:

> Explore using a combination of direct mail with telephone follow-up to ask for bequest gifts. This has been done successfully in Europe.

> Consider organizing free writing of wills for key audiences who are *at risk,* such as new parents and new graduates, using volunteer attorneys. It will be logical for many to include the ABC Organization for a modest percentage-based bequest. This has been done successfully by XYZ Hospital.

> Explore reaching out to newer, younger audiences with vehicles that talk about special opportunities for giving.

3. As part of the board's own commitment to the ABC Organization, board members should be approached for bequest and planned gifts. Current and former board members need to be encouraged to begin exploring how to include ABC in their own estate planning. Each year, an educational session should be conducted. The 120th Anniversary Campaign is a logical reason for emphasizing this *pocket.*

4. As the ABC Organization begins its 120th Anniversary Campaign, planned giving will have a major role in the approach to donors for leadership gifts. At this time it will be logical to create the ABC Planned Giving Resource Advisory Council and to encourage members of the financial community (trust officers, insurance agents, CPAs, realtors, financial planners, and so on) to view the ABC Organization as a resource for clients.

The table titled Major and Planned Giving Strategy summarizes fundraising strategy in these areas for the upcoming fiscal year.

Annual Giving

Annual giving has been viewed by ABC as a series of campaigns (primarily direct mail) rather than as an overall strategy with coordinated steps.

ABC ORGANIZATION: MAJOR AND PLANNED GIVING STRATEGY, FISCAL YEAR 199_

	Strategy	Staff Responsible	Income Goals	Expenses
FIRST HALF OF YEAR: THROUGH DECEMBER 199_			$75,000 outright gifts $300,000 planned gifts	$68,000
General, research, and prospect files	1. Identify top 75 prospects each for end-of-year cultivation; divide by potential.	1. CD, RJ, NT: by 9/15		$2,500
	2. Create survey/executive director letter for top 1,500 prospects.	2. JEN, CD, TS: by 10/15		$1,000
	3. Begin regular internal research through weekly scanning of news media and so on.	3. Adm. asst.: begin 9/15		$2,000 subscriptions
	4. Identify external vendor for overlays, screening	4. JEN: by 9/15		Territory may pick up cost; otherwise $20,000+
	5. Flesh out Donor Circle and Leadership Giving Recognition Program concepts	5. JEN: materials by 11/15 JD: Video by 11/15		$2,500 materials, plaques $8,500 conferences $2,500 memberships
Cultivation and solicitation Current prospects capable of $1,000+	Staff visits	CD, RJ, NT		
Current prospects capable of $250–$999	1. Begin inputting data from survey responses	1. Adm. asst: begin 9/20		
	2. Work through Annual Giving Department for first list for after-marketing approach	2. CD, TS: by 12/31		
Board members	Fiscal year campaign	JEN: begin 9/18; complete by 11/10	$25,000	$500
Acquisitions	1. Begin compiling wish list of $1,000+ prospects	1. All staff: as names surface		$1,500
	2. Begin planned giving public outreach • Column in ABC quarterly newsletter issued in December • Rose Senior Center newsletter, monthly • General planned giving newsletter, to 3,000 • Professionals' charitable intentions newsletter • Advertising	2. CD		$25,000 for entire year

SECOND HALF OF YEAR: JANUARY TO OCTOBER 199_

Category	Activities	Responsible / Timing	Goal	Amount
General, research, and prospect files	Ongoing	Assoc. director	$1,775,000 outright gifts $3,000,000 planned gifts	$62,000
Current prospects capable of $5,000+	1. Ongoing appointments using board and council volunteers	1. JEN: begin 2/9	$100,000 outright gifts	$1,500
	2. Staff-driven solicitations	2. CD: ongoing		$5,000
Current prospects capable of $1,000–$5,000	1. Donor Circle Campaign	1. JEN, CD: begin 1/9	$150,000 outright gifts $2,000,000 planned gifts	$10,000
	2. Donor appreciation event (prior to Community Luncheon)	2. JD: begin 5/9	$1,000,000 outright gifts (goal: 100 donors)	$10,000
Current prospects capable of $250–$999	1. Donor and volunteer appreciation event	1. CD, JD: begin 1/9		$2,000
	2. Telemarketing upgrade campaign	2. CD, TS: begin 3/9		$1,500
Board members	1. Begin appointments and assignments	1. JEN: begin training 1/9	$500,000 (goal: 200 donors) (Under current prospects)	$25,000
	2. Work on own Second Century Campaign gifts	2. JEN: begin 6/9	$500,000 pledges and planned gifts	$1,000
Acquisitions	Begin planned giving public outreach 1. Seminars and speaking • General • Rose Senior Center • Young families: volunteer attorneys write wills • Women: the "sandwiched" generation 2. Advertising 3. Newsletters • Column in ABC quarterly newsletter • Rose Senior Center newsletter, monthly • General planned giving newsletter, to 3,000 • Professionals' charitable intentions newsletter	CD, staff	$50,000	$5,000

There needs to be an interrelation among the areas of creative design, strategy, implementation, gift acknowledgment, donor appreciation, and renewal and upgrading. Without this interrelationship and understanding, it will be impossible for ABC to shift donors from small, fair share giving to more meaningful giving.

• ABC should design a relationship-focused development strategy concentrating on *after marketing*—renewal and upgrading. *A donor who has just made a gift feels good about herself or himself.* Immediately after a gift is made is the best time to approach the donor again with additional information and opportunities for connecting more strongly with the organization. ABC's current support base must continue to be strongly cultivated for renewal and upgrading of gifts. As soon as a gift is made, the cycle of renewed gift giving must begin. Doing this properly requires a strong commitment on the part of the Development Office and the organization.

1. The ABC Organization needs to create an *after-marketing matrix* to maximize donor retention and encourage multiple gifts and upgrading. The after-marketing matrix is a formal multistep program that encourages donors who have made a first gift within the fiscal year to consider a second gift as soon as possible, ideally within the next forty-five days. For the donor who has made a first gift, *the relationship with the organization is just beginning.* The objective of the after-marketing matrix is to respond to this donor position by front-loading cultivation steps and creating a logical climate for a second ask. The matrix offers alternative steps to follow, depending on donor response to the previous steps. Typically it segments donors (minimally) at above and below $100, that is, above and below participation in the Leadership Giving Recognition Program. ABC might also consider segmenting by new, renewing, and upgraded donors and by demographic and psychographic similarities and differences. The usefulness of these segments will depend on the organization's capacity for follow-through and ability to identify these additional criteria in donors.

A generic matrix is shown in the accompanying table, After Marketing: Moving Current Donors Along. ABC will need to decide which specifics work for it, but this sample is a good starting point. The full development staff must be involved in deciding the logical—and doable—steps to encourage strong bonding during the early phase of its donor relationships. It would be useful to hold a meeting to present and discuss the after-marketing concept and to spend time brainstorming specifics.

2. Currently, the acknowledgment and appreciation cycle is inadequate; in some cases it is almost nonexistent. Although the development staff have indicated their commitment to getting acknowledgments out speedily, the reality is that this does not usually happen. Several of the donors inter-

viewed for this assessment mentioned their concerns regarding lack of acknowledgment and appreciation for their gifts. Accountability must be assigned for this goal. Recommended steps include the following:

Acknowledgment letters must be updated each month to be timely. Each letter should contain a P.S. asking for an action step (making an endorsement that the organization can use in its communications, completing an enclosed survey, making an additional gift, upgrading the level of membership, considering a planned gift, and so on).

SAMPLE MATRIX: AFTER MARKETING: MOVING CURRENT DONORS ALONG

Matrix A: All Donors After the First Gift in the Fiscal Year

First Gift of Year	In 48 Hours	In 7 Days	In 15 Days	In 30 Days	In 45 Days
Under $100	Thank-you letter with receipt	Donor survey	Leadership Giving Recognition Program invitation	*If no gift*, specialized mailer (see Matrix B if a gift is made)	*If no gift*, return to general database for contact in 3 months
$100+ donors	Thank-you letter with Leadership Giving Recognition Program member packet	Thank-you phone call; *try to set appointment for gifts over $250*	Welcome packet • Survey • Fact sheet • Magazine or annual report • Business card	Partners (monthly giving) invitation	*If no gift*, specialized mailer (see Matrix B if a gift is made)

Matrix B: Donors Renewing Within the Fiscal Year

Additional Gift Within Year	In 48 Hours	In 7 Days	In 15 Days	In 30 Days	In 45 Days
Nonpartners with total gifts of $100	Thank-you letter ("Why do I give?"); survey (if not previously returned)	Thank-you phone call by staff	Partners (monthly giving) invitation	*If no gift*, specialized mailer	*If no gift*, return to database for telephone contact within 3 months
Nonpartners with total gifts of $100+	Thank-you letter with Partners packet	Thank-you phone call; *try to set appointment for gifts over $250*	Partners (monthly giving) invitation	*If no gift*, specialized mailer	*If no gift*, return to database for telephone contact within 3 months

Matrix C: Ongoing Pledges

Multiple Donor	48 Hours After Receipt	7 Days After Receipt	15 Days Before First Payment Due	15 Days After Receipt
All	Thank-you letter	Thank-you call	Pledge payment request; thank-you letter	Bank draft invitation

Note: All donors are added to the quarterly ABC newsletter subscriber list.

A new donor welcome packet should be created (an oversized 9-by-12-inch envelope with "Thank You" or "Urgent: Donor Information" emblazoned on it) to be sent to first-time donors (either all or a segment of them, such as those giving $100 or more). The packet might consist of

A donor survey

A copy of the most recent newsletter

A fact sheet or overview brochure

The business card of a contact person in the Development Office

Each thank-you should be as personalized as possible. The ABC Organization has a large number of retired staff and volunteers who could be asked to handwrite thank-you letters or telephone donors at the $100 level and above.

3. ABC needs to rebuild relations with many of its current annual donors. Several of those interviewed have mentioned the problems in the mid-1980s when ABC became overextended. The consensus is that many donors became unhappy with ABC and either stopped giving or held their gifts to modest levels.

The giving histories do not reflect increased support from donors. Current modest donors need to be encouraged to feel that they are part of a family. By asking their assistance, providing them with information and feedback, and responding quickly to their needs, ABC will create a stronger bond with them. Specific recommended steps include using a supporter survey and redesigning the reply envelope to encourage donors to indicate how ABC can serve them better.

ABC should encourage, via a monthly pledging program, individuals whose giving has been at $99 or less to upgrade to—at least—$100. This will require a specific strategy, using a combination of direct mail and telemarketing. Initially, ABC should identify those who have given three gifts in two years and contact them as a group; beginning in March 1998, ABC should include this strategy as a general step in its after-marketing matrix.

Finally, ABC has internal audiences who may not view themselves as *donors* but who can also be moved along and should be included on ABC's after-marketing matrix. They include persons who make small contributions, who could be encouraged to provide names, addresses, and phone numbers for future follow-up, as well as memorial and tribute donors who make gifts in memory or in honor of individuals. The latter often have no personal interest in giving to ABC; the organization is the recipient of their tribute, not the cause of it. These donors rarely give again because their commitment is to the honoree, not the charity. However, this does not have to be the case. ABC should develop a specific strategy that acknowledges that the memorial or tribute donor needs to make a conscious decision to become a real donor and that provides steps to encourage that decision.

• ABC must be more active in turning lapsed donors into renewing donors and in preventing donors from lapsing. Although it has proven impossible to get accurate figures, the Annual Giving Department estimates that the annual donor renewal rate is less than 60 percent. This translates into ABC's losing over 40 percent of its donors each year and needing to find replacements just to remain stable in its private support.

Although the number one goal should be not to lose donors, the second goal should be to reconnect those who have dropped off. It takes five times as much work to find a new donor and get him or her to begin giving as to retain or reactivate an existing donor. As soon as a gift is made, the cycle of renewed gift giving must begin. Recognition and appreciation needs to be done on a regular basis.

Often lost donors need only to hear they are missed to reactivate the cycle of giving. However, this strategy must be personalized. It has already been recommended (under major giving) that in-person visits be made to reconnect donors who gave in the past. When this is not possible, especially for donors of smaller gifts, lapsed donors should be approached with a combined direct-mail and phone campaign.

This approach requires a computerized *flagging* system:

1. Identify donors who have not given a second gift nine months into the year. Visit or send a personalized appeal letter followed by a phone call thanking the donor for past support, updating him or her on the year's progress, and asking for a commitment.

2. At the one-year anniversary (assuming no gift has yet been made), automatically activate a "we miss you" strategy (possibly a letter and a phone call).

• ABC needs a focus on acquisition. Its current donor base is aging. Even if ABC increases its renewal rates to 90 percent or more, over time it must find new donors. It makes the most sense to look for middle-aged (boomer) and young adult (buster) audiences. To date, ABC's acquisition efforts have proven expensive because the results are poor. Therefore, ABC should differentiate between general acquisition (bringing in large numbers of individuals at any level of first-time giving as cost effectively as possible) and selective acquisition (choosing specific, logical audiences for acquisition at higher giving levels).

1. To improve general acquisition, ABC should explore alternatives to its traditional use of direct mail. Television and space ads need to be considered. A truly interactive Web site should be created to encourage visits from younger and technologically oriented individuals. Once donors are acquired, they should move rapidly into the after-marketing matrix for renewal and upgrading.

2. ABC should concentrate on selective acquisition, acquiring affluent individuals who are capable of making gifts of $100 and more. The goal should be penetration: pick a segment and go deep rather than wide. It will be better to bring in 1,000 new donors with a commitment to giving $1,000 and more per year than to bring in 100,000 new donors giving $10 or even 10,000 giving $100. The costs are much less per donor acquired, and the smaller numbers will give ABC the opportunity to forge stronger relationships.

As ABC concentrates on middle-aged boomers and young adult busters in the metro vicinity and statewide, it might be logical to test the following lists:

Professionals in Health and Human Services

Social workers

Mental health practitioners

Physical and occupational therapists

Educators

Gerontologists

Persons and Groups Committed to Social Justice

Churches

Liberal political organizations; EMILY's List

Women without children, in their forties and early fifties

Donors to the American Civil Liberties Union (ACLU), Southern Poverty Law Center, Amnesty International, and so forth

ABC should also try to locate newcomers to its community. These individuals, especially those who have purchased homes, are in transition. This is an opportunity for ABC to present itself as a good community partner, offering help along with an invitation to get involved.

The Annual Giving Strategy recommends an annual giving plan for ABC.

Special Events

Successful major dollar special event fundraising requires a constituency of high potential, a strong chair or committee, and a gap in the community calendar of events. Events are either for friend raising, where the goal is to involve large numbers of volunteers and participants for image-building reasons, or fundraising, where the goal is to raise large dollars as efficiently as possible.

The ABC Organization has two major fundraising events: the Golf Outing and the Community Luncheon. Each of ABC's fundraising events was evaluated carefully in terms of its potential for raising additional monies in the years ahead, that is, actual income versus expenses.

• The Golf Outing is approaching its tenth year. Although accurate records are difficult to find, actual dollars raised appear to have deteriorated sharply while attendance has grown only modestly. This year, just $10,000 was raised (compared to $15,000 two years previously), while costs have increased steadily over the years. As a result, only $1,500 net was realized from the most recent event.

In addition, volunteers and staff associated with the event noted that

Clear goals do not exist.

There is no ownership by the volunteers.

There is poor communication between volunteers and staff.

Staff are not perceived as supportive.

The Golf Outing should be discontinued as quickly as possible.

• The Community Luncheon is in its fourth year, bringing in approximately $131,000 against costs of $40,000, a net gain of $91,000. Last year's attendance was 450 persons (compared to 400 the previous year). The event provides ABC with excellent community outreach and is viewed positively by volunteers, staff, and attendees.

Additional efforts should be put into growing the Community Luncheon further as it is an outstanding cultivation event. The event committee should look at expanding the underwriting and sponsorship opportunities.

• Various program departments hold fundraising events (coupon book sales, greeting cards, and so on). They produce modest fundraising results ($2,000 to $5,000) and require little work on the part of the organization. *As long as these department efforts continue to be viewed as "fun" by volunteers, they can be continued but should be monitored carefully.*

• ABC needs to develop some events that cultivate new audiences. The Hispanic community, for example, appears unaware of ABC's role and

ABC ORGANIZATION: ANNUAL GIVING STRATEGY

Strategy	Staff Responsible	Income Goals	Expenses
THROUGH DECEMBER 199_		$1,100,000	$170,000
Database management			$5,000 bank costs
Donors $1–$249	1. JEN, TS: by 12/26	$150,000	$32,000
1. Quarterly newsletter 30,000; all local donors			
2. Thanksgiving and Christmas appeals	2. TS: by 10/9 and 12/9	$950,000	$90,000
Acquisitions			
1. Space ads			
• Thanksgiving			$4,600
• Christmas			$7,000
2. Newspaper inserts			$9,400
Gift acknowledgment			$12,000
JANUARY–OCTOBER 199_		$2,185,000	$404,000
Database management			$5,000 postage due
			$3,500 corps training
			$12,500 lock box fees
Donors $1–$99	1. JEN, TS: outside vendor	$600,000	$150,000
1. Telemarketing programs 30,000 names			
• New donor welcome programs			
Christmas			
1/9 and on			
All making second gift			
No second gift			
• Monthly giving program: 2 gifts in year; 3+ years of giving			
• Lapsed donor program: 25–36 months; 8,000 names			
• Donors acquired through past telemarketing program			

Donors $100–$249	2. Quarterly newsletter 30,000 metro area 150,000 statewide	2. JEN, TS: by 3/9, 6/9, 9/9	$150,000 $100,000	$50,000 $56,000
	3. Quarterly seasonal theme mailings	3. TS: by 1/9, 4/9, 7/9	$200,000	$40,000
	4. Special appeals	4. TS: by 5/9, 8/9	$50,000	$10,000
	Upgrade to Donor Circle: 5,000 names	JEN, TS: outside vendor	$1,000,000	$100,000
Conversions	1. Memorial or tribute donors	TS		
	2. Disaster donors			
	3. Events audiences			
Acquisitions	1. Pinpointed ($100 potential): 50,000 names	1. JN, TS	$50,000	$27,500
	2. Newspaper inserts	2. TS	$35,000	$10,500
Gift acknowledgment				$25,000
TOTAL			$3,185,000	$589,000

contains some significant pockets of affluence. *A committee to investigate the potential for a new event, with the emphasis on cultivation rather than solicitation, should be formed.*

Corporate and Foundation Relations

Increasingly, private foundations are focusing their dollars on a few key organizations instead of spreading them out with little impact in any one area. But ABC has not used its position as a leading not-for-profit to maximize its share of the grants that are available. It has been reactive rather than proactive. Grants that have been realized are exceedingly modest and do not reflect ABC's stature in the community.

- The funding community demonstrates a lack of understanding of ABC's financial situation and its need for funding partners. As part of the assessment's information gathering, two foundations that have made small but steady gifts to ABC's domestic violence program were visited. Neither appeared aware of the scope of the program ABC offers. Appointments need to be set up with current and immediate past funders to help them meet ABC's leadership and better understand ABC's value to the community.

- Program department heads are unaware of grant opportunities. Or, in effect, they compete for the same funding dollars. Program department heads are deciding for themselves which funders to approach, often receiving small gifts because they are not matching their programs well with available grants. A system of sign-offs must be implemented that matches organizational priorities with funders. ABC has not gone back to funders on an annual basis, asking them to give again and give more. A tracking system needs to be implemented to make sure funding deadlines are not missed.

- ABC should seek out partnerships with other not-for-profits, businesses, and community partners to produce *synergies.* Increasingly, not-for-profits are being told by foundations that the foundations view themselves as seeding innovative programs to demonstrate cooperation among not-for-profits in the community rather than as providing ongoing support for a particular organization's established programs and services. Family foundations are now being taken over by a completely new generation with new ideas of funding priorities; many times they are no longer loyal to the city where their families' wealth originated. ABC's executive director should be introduced to his counterparts and should engage in dialogue with them to seek out innovative solutions to needs. ABC should take the leadership in putting together proposals for not-for-profit *consortiums.*

- Realistic new sources of grants should be explored. Using the *Foundation Databook* for the state, Oregon's Grant Consultant database, and also materials available through the Foundation Center, application materials and guidelines should be gathered from all logical funding prospects. An internal newsletter—distributed quarterly—would communicate this source information efficiently.

• Corporate giving out of the charitable pocket is declining. Corporations have moved from giving to charity to funding cause-related marketing to sponsoring socially responsible partnerships. Increasingly, major corporations are looking for opportunities that will involve long-term commitments on both sides. Corporations will be seeking out not-for-profit partners that can (a) provide services for their employees or customers, thus enabling them to be more competitive, and (b) provide far-reaching positive publicity through name linkage. For example, the "IJK Company" is relocating its corporate headquarters to Oregon, and this is an opportunity for ABC. A strategy should be created to address such opportunities.

1. ABC should work with other not-for-profits to encourage corporations and smaller businesses to extend or add, as employee benefits, matching gift programs that include human and social service organizations. More and more, corporations are finding their philanthropic decisions challenged by stockholders, employees, and the community at large. An argument can be easily made for the *safety* in using corporate charitable dollars to also provide an employee benefit. Although educational institutions have benefited significantly from this rationale, other not-for-profits have not been perceived as worthy beneficiaries. This is largely because they have not lobbied for the benefits they produce the way higher education has via the Council for the Support and Advancement of Education.

2. Workplace giving is moving in new directions. There are three reasons for this: the employee pool, no longer made up largely of the *civic* generations, is now less interested in pleasing employers; there are fewer traditional Fortune 100 companies, due to mergers and acquisitions; and newly formed companies are tending to be entrepreneurial, with smaller numbers of employees and without the infrastructure to support employee campaigns. As United Way, in its May 1995 *Strategic Planning Report,* notes: "an increasing portion of businesses are service, professional or technology-based organizations with a more decentralized, empowered employee approach for which traditional workplace campaigns have been less effective."

Employee-directed giving is increasingly taking place via alternative campaigns. The ABC Organization should consider whether it needs to lobby in conjunction with other human services and public benefit–focused charities for the ability to offer such campaigns in the workplace.

Where ABC can identify its United Way designated donors, it should make it a priority to cultivate these individuals for continued and increased giving. They should be put into a specific after-marketing matrix.

Conclusion

The ABC Organization is to be applauded for its vision in facing the future and in exploring measures that will position it to remain strong and viable in meeting its commitments through its fundraising. Now the organization must position the Development Office to succeed. The cost (both in terms of credibility and dollars) is too great to allow failure.

Recommended Steps for Implementation: Timeline

Moving from the current paradigm will require a strong commitment on the part of everyone at ABC. First, those who have been less committed to fundraising will have to accept it as an organizational priority. Then those in the Development Office must have a willingness to guide ABC leadership, volunteers, program staff.

Once ownership is agreed to, strategy must be outlined, and a realistic development budget must be developed. Finally, there must be implementation. Setting forth a proposed strategy will get you only halfway there; making sure that the various pieces of the strategy actually happen is equally—if not more—important.

The proposed timeline indicates timing and accountability very specifically. This is a very aggressive timeline. However, it is attainable. The strategy proceeds from concerns about implementing any major fundraising changes during the last quarter of the calendar year, as it is during that quarter, from October through December, that typically 70 percent of ABC's private support is raised. Therefore, it is recommended that major program changes occur after the first of January 199_.

INTRODUCTORY PHASE: FIRST SIX MONTHS, JANUARY–JUNE 1998

Conduct development assessment (January–March 1998)

- Present draft report to executive director and president of board (March 1998)
- Finalize report (March 1998)

Provide the opportunity for formal and informal gatekeepers to take ownership of the recommendations in the development assessment (March–April 1998)

- Debrief board
- Debrief ABC staff leadership
- Debrief development staff

Restructure Office of Development (May–July 1998)

- Review and upgrade staffing as necessary

  Create job descriptions for newly organized department slots

  Evaluate current development staff

  Hire new staff as needed

  Set training schedule(s) for computer, fundraising

- Refine two-year development strategy and budget for each development area

  Strategies and budgets outlined by each department (by June 15)

  Approved by ABC (July 31)

Develop Development Office protocols, procedures, and systems (May–July 1998)

- Complete gift stewardship and accountability guidelines

- Create performance reports

- Create after-marketing and acknowledgment steps

IMPLEMENTATION STAGE: SEPTEMBER–DECEMBER 1998

Create general brochures, materials, and reply envelopes

- Formulate case statement and vital needs

- Develop Leadership Giving Recognition Program materials

  Begin to develop video(s)

  Identify vendors for telemarketing and printing

  Create newsletter format

Conduct annual board, faculty, and staff campaigns (August–September 1998)

Continue end-of-calendar-year annual giving appeals with minor modifications

Move toward major giving
orientation

- Begin prospect research of
  current donors
  Create donor survey
  Begin in-house research using
  other organizations' annual
  reports, public information
  Review possible screening packages
- Begin to hold regular meetings
  and focus groups with prospects
  and funders capable of gifts of
  $1,000+
- Formalize funding needs and
  concept of 120th Anniversary
  Campaign

ROLLOUT: JANUARY–SEPTEMBER 1999

Begin use of after-marketing
matrix

Move to new quarterly
newsletter schedule

Implement grant-writing
newsletter and schedule

Implement revised annual giving
strategy for renewal and
upgrading, lapsed, and
acquisition donor segments

Implement Donor Circle strategy
for midlevel major giving

Resources: Supporting Materials

Resource A: Responsibilities of the Board (Sample Job Description)

The board of trustees of the ABC Organization enables the organization to
cultivate and solicit the private support dollars needed for fulfillment of its
mission. Board members' responsibilities include

- Setting and approving development goals and objectives
- Being an advocate for the organization and actively assisting in giv-
  ing and getting
- Exercising gift stewardship and accountability

More specifically, each board member exemplifies these characteristics:

1. Commitment to the goals, objectives, and services of the ABC Organization:

   Attends board planning retreats and orientation sessions

   Attends quarterly meetings regularly

   Makes a meaningful annual gift

2. Willingness and ability to act as a spokesperson for the ABC Organization with potential contributors:

   Articulates ABC's goals and objectives to those capable of financially supporting it

   Promotes ABC to personal, business, media, and other public and private contacts

   Assists in identifying persons and entities capable of financially supporting ABC

   Expresses appreciation—through visits, personal notes, and telephone calls—to those who support ABC

3. Willingness and ability to assist in securing adequate finances for the ABC Organization by ensuring personal, firm, corporate, or service club support and the support of friends. Each board member has the responsibility to give or secure a minimum of $5,000 annually each year.

   Assists in the cultivation of key prospects

   Accompanies others in solicitation visits

   Participates in major benefit functions and special events

Resource B: Sample Gift Stewardship and Accountability Guidelines

The following stewardship and accountability guidelines are offered as a starting point for the ABC Organization's own comprehensive set of guidelines. They are based on sample guidelines in Judith E. Nichols's *Targeted Fund Raising: Defining and Refining Your Development Strategy* (Chicago: Precept Press, 1991). Not all areas in this sample document may ultimately be found relevant. The purpose of these guidelines is to provide a structure for board, staff, volunteers, and donors that answers commonly asked questions about the ABC Organization's policies for private contributions.

1. *Who can accept gifts on behalf of ABC?* Unrestricted gifts of cash in any amount may be accepted by the executive director, the directors of the various departments on behalf of their particular areas of responsibility, the development director, and members of the ABC Development Council on behalf of the organization.

Noncash and restricted gifts of $1,000 or less may be accepted by the executive director, the directors of the various departments on behalf of their particular areas of responsibility, the development director, and members of the ABC Development Council on behalf of the organization.

All noncash and restricted gifts of over $1,000 are reviewed for approval by the Finance Committee of the board of the ABC Organization. The review will be scheduled within a 45-day period.

2. *What types of gifts are accepted by ABC?* Gifts are defined as follows:

- *Unrestricted:* gifts of any amount without donor qualifications as to use

- *Designated:* gifts of over $100 directed to a general area of interest, such as a department or program

- *Restricted:* gifts of over $1,000 with donor restrictions as to program or service usage

The ABC Organization accepts gifts of cash; securities; irrevocable planned gift arrangements using bequests, life insurance, trusts, and annuities; and in-kind and real property contributions, using the following guidelines:

- Stock gifts are attributed their median price on the day received.

- Gifts of real property valued at $5,000 and over should be evaluated by an independent appraiser. The ABC Organization does not assign a value for tax purposes to noncash contributions, although it will assign a general *internal* level for donor recognition.

- Pledges paid within a five-year period are assigned full current value. Until paid in full, they are considered accounts receivable and assigned 70 percent of value.

- Deferred gifts (including but not limited to annuities, unitrusts, pooled income vehicles, and irrevocable bequests) are assigned a value adjusted for current value using actuarial tables for the age of the donor.

- Bequests that are revocable are assigned a value of $1,000. If the actual amount is known it is recorded for an *internal* level of donor recognition only.

3. *What forms of donor recognition does ABC give?* All gifts to the ABC Organization are sincerely appreciated and promptly acknowledged with a letter.

Unless a donor requests anonymity, all contributors for the immediate past fiscal year are listed in the annual report or an honor roll of donors.

Donors who contribute at and above $100 become participants in ABC's Donor Circles, with these levels of membership:

Members	$100 to $999 in annual gifts
Contributors	$1,000 to $9,999 in annual gifts
Benefactors	$10,000 and above in cumulative gifts
Key Club	Bequests and other planned gifts

A personalized certificate of appreciation is provided to members of the Donor Circles upon request.

Donors who indicate in writing that they have included the ABC Organization or a particular department in their will or other planned giving vehicle become members of the Key Club. No amount need be specified.

4. *How does ABC recover fundraising costs from contributions?* The ABC Organization raises funds on behalf of the organization and its entities through an intensified development strategy, using personal solicitations, corporate and foundation proposals, direct mail, telecommunications, and special events.

All direct costs for fundraising are recovered from these efforts before funds are distributed.

Twenty percent of each undesignated gift is assigned to the Office of Development to cover the costs of fundraising.

For designated or restricted gifts, direct costs of fundraising are recovered by the following formula:

- Ten percent levy for gifts of up to $100,000
- Five percent levy for gifts of over $100,000

This levy can be paid in any of the following ways:

- With donor agreement, taken from the gift
- With donor agreement, supplementing the gift
- With board agreement, taken from another source of revenue, including unrestricted and designated funds or existing endowment monies

After fundraising costs are recovered, the ABC Organization allocates the remaining unrestricted dollars among its entities and departments. Recommendations for distribution will be made quarterly by the Administrators' Council.

5. *What levels of funding does ABC require for a named endowment?* A sum of $10,000 or more establishes a named endowment fund. The first grant is made during the July following the completion of the first full fiscal year after the fund's establishment. The grant is limited to 5 percent of the interest income, with the remaining interest going back into the endowment to build principal.

6. *What levels of funding does ABC require for trusts and annuities?* The sum of $50,000 establishes a charitable remainder trust or annuity. Generally, these trusts and annuities are made available to individuals aged fifty-five or older. Up to two beneficiaries may be named to receive payments. The trust or annuity must be funded with a vehicle that can be readily liquidated prior to payments commencing.

7. *What are ABC's requirements for bequest gifts?* Bequest gifts of any amount are welcome. Because it is difficult to anticipate the needs of the future, donors are requested to leave their bequest gifts to the ABC Organization unrestricted or designated rather than restricted.

8. *What in-kind donations does ABC accept?* Limited amounts of office equipment, durable goods, and specific materials in good condition are needed, subject to the approval of the Finance Committee, as described earlier. In-kind gifts are assigned no value by the ABC Organization. It is the responsibility of the donor to obtain a valuation for tax purposes.

9. *What are ABC's policies for sponsorship, cause-related marketing, premiums, and incentives?* The ABC Organization recognizes that its name carries weight in the community. Before agreeing to lend ABC's implied endorsement to a for-profit entity through sponsorship or cause-related marketing, the Sponsorship Committee will meet, review the request, and advise the board. A decision will be rendered within 45 days of the request.

Fundraising appeals that in exchange for a contribution offer premiums or incentives (the value of which is not insubstantial but is significant in relation to the amount of the contribution) will advise the donor of the fair market value of the premium or incentive and that the value is not deductible for tax purposes.

10. *What are ABC's investment policies?* As an ethical, responsible member of the community, the ABC Organization will not invest in stock and bond vehicles that either directly or indirectly refute its mission. These include stocks and bonds in companies that deal with tobacco and alcohol products and companies with a history of discriminating by race and ethnicity, age, gender, or sexual orientation. ABC does not do business with countries that ignore the civil rights of their citizens.

11. *What is ABC's stance on the use of commission-based fundraising consultants?* ABC subscribes to the principles of both the American Association of Fund-Raising Counsel and the National Society of Fund Raising Executives. It does not hire fundraisers on a percentage basis.

12. *What is ABC's stance on donor privacy?* ABC recognizes that donors are at the heart of the organization's viability and that it has strong responsibilities to protect their privacy. For example,

- All donors are contacted prior to the printing of the annual honor roll in the September issue of the quarterly newsletter and advised that names are being listed. Donors are given the option of remaining anonymous.

- Donors are welcome to request and receive a complete copy of any written materials held in their file.

- Only authorized staff and board members may view a donor file.

- Donor files remain on site.

Appendixes

Appendix A: Program and Service Needs Assessment Results

Appendix B: List of Participants

Appendix C: List of Materials Requested and Gathered

Appendix D: Copy of the Development Assessment Survey[3]

Appendix A: Program and Service Needs Assessment Results

The first step in creating a long-range development strategy is always to define what must be raised and to match these needs with the groups of donors most likely to have interest in these needs and the ability to fund them.

The accompanying Summary and Breakdown of Fundraising Requirements demonstrates very roughly the dollars that ABC must raise for overall organizational needs and also for the needs of a number of individual programs.

Directors of as many program areas as possible were asked to provide a rough estimate of what *additional funding* would be necessary to bring

---

3. The development assessment survey is not included in this example. A sample survey is shown in full in Chapter Seven.

ABC ORGANIZATION: SUMMARY AND BREAKDOWN OF FUNDRAISING REQUIREMENTS

	Needed Currently	Three to Five Years Out	Five to Ten Years Out
OVERALL			
Operating needs	$3,439,909.60	$4,371,875	$5,267,585
Capital needs	$344,000.00	$13,610,000	$9,075,000
Total operating and capital needs	$3,783,909.60	$17,981,875	$14,342,585
Endowment needs	$1,000,000.00	$6,000,000	$15,000,000
BREAKDOWN BY INDIVIDUAL CENTERS			
ABC SCHOOL (provided by Ann S.)			
Operating needs	$50,000.00	$50,000	$100,000
Capital needs		$100,000	
ABC STREET YOUTH PROGRAM (provided by Ann S.)			
Operating needs	$560,000.00	$700,000	$100,000 $350,000 staff $250,000 new initiatives $1,750,000 group homes
Capital needs		$2,500,000 facility	
ABC TEEN PARENTING PROGRAM (provided by Roger L.)			
Operating needs	$120,000.00	$136,800	$140,000
Capital needs		$800,000 day care facility	$200,000 repairs
EXTENSION SERVICES (provided by Bob T.)			
Operating needs	$392,750.00	$600,000	$1,000,000
Capital needs		$500,000: 2 core sites	$3,000,000: 6 to 8 core sites
ALCOHOL REHABILITATION SERVICES (provided by John S.)			
Operating needs	$1,425,504.00	$1,625,075	$1,852,585
Capital needs		$7,500,000	
FAMILY SERVICES (provided by Robin G.)			
Operating needs	$250,000.00	$400,000 $150,000 staff	$1,000,000
Capital needs		$750,000 warehouse	$2,000,000 to $3,000,000 programs

ABC COMMUNITY CENTER (provided by Rick J.)			
Operating needs	$408,000.00	$500,000	$600,000
Capital needs	$125,000.00 repairs $65,000.00 staff	$250,000 repairs $1,100,000 land acquisition and facility	$100,000 repairs $175,000 staff
WOMEN'S PROGRAMS (provided by Nancy D.)			
Operating needs	(Currently fully funded by DHQ) $50,000.00 staff	$60,000	$75,000
Capital needs			
THE RESOURCE CENTER (provided by Penny L.)			
Operating needs	$83,665.63 $15,000.00 freezer 34,000.00 truck 13,000.00 forklift		
Capital needs			
ABC SENIOR CENTER (provided by Jennifer M.)			
Operating needs	$150,000.00	$300,000	$400,000
Capital needs	$42,000 staff	$2,000,000 facility $50,000 staff	$250,000 new outreach programs

Note:

Operating needs: unrestricted funding for programs and services that are offered on an ongoing basis. Includes staffing and operational costs (rent, materials, and so forth). Best served by gifts from donors who are willing to let the organization determine the *area of greatest need. Target audiences:* those who may give repeating (annual) gifts of smaller amounts.

Capital needs: restricted funding for specific projects or programs that arise as special needs. Includes facility building and renovation, equipment purchase and upgrading, and so forth. *Target audiences:* those who may give one-time gifts of, typically, $1,000 and more.

Endowment needs: unrestricted and restricted funding that creates a *safety net* for the organization. Typically recommended as the capital needed to produce 20 percent of the operating needs. *Target audiences:* those who may give bequest and life income gifts.

their area of responsibility to a funding level that restores the cuts made during ABC's financial crisis (see the "Needed Currently" column). Each director was then asked to project out for the near future (three to five years) and for the long term (ten years out). Fees for service and any ensured income were factored out. However, the contribution from national headquarters was included.

Appendix B: List of Participants

On behalf of the ABC Organization, sincere thanks to all participants.

Internal	**External**
Administrative Leadership	Corporate Contributions Director, FGH Bank
Executive Director	Community Relations, CDE Utilities
Chief Logistics Officer	Executive Director, LMN Foundation
CFO	CEO, United Way
MIS Director	
Program Leadership	Executive directors and fundraising executives from a number of charities similar to the ABC Organization were asked for opinions in the course of this assessment.
City Programs Coordinator	
Women's Program Director	
Alcohol Rehabilitation Services Director	
Service Extension Director	Several current and past major donors to ABC graciously agreed to be interviewed. In the interest of protecting their privacy, their names are not recorded in this document.
Family Services Director	
Community Center Director	
Domestic Violence Shelter Director	
Teen Parenting Director	
Street Youth Director	
Senior Center Director	

Board Leadership
Board of Trustees President
Current Board Members
Emeritus Board Members

Development Department Staff
Development Director
Major Giving Director
Planned Giving Director
Annual Giving Director

Support Staff
Grant Writer

Appendix C: List of Materials Requested and Gathered

ABC ORGANIZATION: LIST OF MATERIALS REQUESTED AND RECEIVED

Information Requested	Status	Individual Responsible
Development staff job descriptions	Received: institutional versions	David H.
Development staff résumés	—	Administrative assistant (open)
	Received	George B.
	Received	Deborah J.
	Received	Tim R.
	Not received	Candy P.
	Received	Joe W.
	Received	Cheryl D.
	Received	Linda R.
	Not received	Karen B.
	Received	Maria F.
	Not received	Donna G.
	Not received	Kim L.
	Not received	Judith M.
Board of trustees and councils		
Evaluation of giving, getting, political clout	Received	Victoria T.
Thumbnail bios of board members	Received	
Special events	Not received	Victoria T.
List of events held regularly, with (for each one) $$ raised, month held, short explanation of what it is, who runs it, who benefits		
Community Luncheon		
Golf Outing		
Others?		
Development reports		
End-of-year development statistics	Not received	Justin C.
What came in, monthly by category		
Listing of number of donors at each $$ level of giving from highest to lowest		
Spreadsheets showing 12-month activity		
Annual giving	Not received	Karen B.
Planned giving	Received	Deborah J.
Donor analysis (renewal percent)	Not received	Karen B.
Tracking form for planned gifts	Received	Deborah J.
Guidelines		
Grants	Received	Cheryl D.
Planned giving		Deborah J.
Donor appreciation strategy		
Planned giving	Not received	Deborah J.
Program areas		
Senior center	Done	Jennifer M.
Street youth program/school	Done	Ann S.
Teen parenting	Done	Roger L.
Extension	Done	Bob T.
Alcohol rehabilitation	Done	John S.
Domestic violence shelter	Done	Dana W.
Resource center	To be sent	Penny L.
Women's programs	Done	Nancy D.
Family services	Telemarketing brochure	Robin G.

Index

A

Accountability: sample guidelines on, 127–129, 163–167; survey questions on, 84–85

Acknowledgment. *See* Gift acknowledgment

Affluent market: advantages of fundraising among, 47; annual income of, 45; increasing size of, 45–46

After-marketing matrix strategy, 47–48; in sample report, 150, 151

Age groups: diversity among, 33–35; in sample report, 119. *See also specific age groups*

Albrecht, K., 24

American Association of Fund-Raising Counsel, 27, 45

Analysis of Demographic Data for Top 100 Donors: directions for, 79; sample form, 83

Annual giving: from affluent market, 46–47; in sample report, 147, 150–154, 156–157; survey questions on, 91–92

Asian Americans, demographic trends among, 32–33

Assessment coordinator, 8–9, 66

Assessment folder, 63

Assessment survey, 12, 66; assessment folder for documents from, 63; form for recording information from, 66–70; general directions for, 66; record-keeping forms for, 63–66; sample, 71–98

B

Baby boomers: age and number of, 31; communication preferences of, 38; individual giving by, 40, 41; philanthropic personality of, 34, 35, 40; in sample report, 119

Baby boomlets: globalism of, 40; philanthropic personality of, 34–35

Baby busters: communication preferences of, 38; number of, 31; philanthropic personality of, 34, 35; in sample report, 119

Barker, J., 24

Black Americans, demographic trends among, 33

Board of trustees: chair of, 9, 13; debriefing, 19; financial commitment by, 44, 125; importance of support of, 8; resources on, 58; sample job description for, 162–163; in sample report, 122–126; survey questions for, 75–76

Boomers. *See* Baby boomers

Boomlets. *See* Baby boomlets

Budget, in sample report, 113, 135–136. *See also* Income and expenses

Busters. *See* Baby busters

C

Capital needs, 74, 109, 118

Chair of board: communication by, 9; interview with, 13

Change, 23–26; constancy of, 23–24; and environmental scanning, 25–26; reaction to, 24; in sample report, 103–104; shifting paradigms with, 24–25

Charitable Better Business Bureau (CBBB), 137

Checklist for Data Collection: directions for, 63; sample form, 64–65

Communication: gender differences in, 36; matching prospects with methodology for, 38, 44

Community members, gathering information from, 14–15

Computers: communication methodology variety with, 38; globalism with, 40; in sample report, 134–135; survey questions on, 84

Consultants, development assessments conducted by, 7

Cornish, E., 23

Corporate giving: resources on, 59; in sample report, 158–159; survey questions on, 92; trends in, 28–29

Council for Advancement and Support of Education (CASE), 130

D

De Pree, M., 4

Debriefings, 18–19

Demographic trends, 29–38; diversity, 31–37; as environmental scan element, 25–26; and fundraising strategies, 38; and lifestyle and life stage, 37; longevity, 30–31, 37; resources on, 52–56, 60; in sample report, 118–120; survey questions on, 71

Depression babies, philanthropic personality of, 34, 35, 39

Development assessment: areas reviewed in, 6, 7; commitment to, 8–9;

debriefing component of, 18–19; follow-up work on, 20; information gained from, 3–5; interview component of, 12–15; organization-wide support for, 8, 9; selecting person to conduct, 7; timeline for, 6, 9, 19; when to conduct, 5–6; written report on, 15–18. *See also* Assessment survey

Development assessment report, 15–18; general format for, 16–18. *See also* Sample report

Development committee, in sample report, 126–127

Development office: budget for, 135–136; reorganizing, in sample report, 130–138

Direct mail: for communicating with prospects, 38, 44; resources on, 59

Director of development: in organizational chart, 133; survey questions for, 94

Directors. *See* Board of trustees

Diversity, 31–37; age-group, 33–35; gender, in communication, 36; lifestyle and life stage, 37; racial/ethnic, 31–33; in sample report, 119

Donor pyramid, 37, 47

Donors: acquisition of, 139, 140, 153–154; enlarged base of, 47; lybnt, 44; renewal of, 47–48, 139, 140; survey questions on, 79, 81, 83; sybnt, 44; upgrading of, 139. *See also* Prospects

E

Edie, D. C., 26

Endowment needs, 74, 109, 118

Environmental scanning, 25–26; on fundraising, 56–62; internal resources for, 51; on national trends, 52–54; on regional and local trends, 54–56

Executive director: communication by, 9; importance of support of, 8; interview with, 13; role of, 129–130; survey questions for, 76

F

Financial Needs: assessment of, 167–170; directions for listing, 74; sample form, 74; in sample report, 109, 117–118, 167–170; survey questions on, 74–75

Flagging system, donor, 153

Focus groups, 14–15

Form for Recording Survey Information: directions for, 66; sample form, 67–70

Foundation giving: resources on, 59; in sample report, 158–159; survey questions on, 92; trends in, 28

Fundraising: expense ratios for, 137; resources on, 56–62; survey questions on, 77–97

Fundraising History: directions for completing, 77; sample form, 78

Fundraising strategies: assumptions underlying, 43–48; and demographic trends, 38; focused, 138–140; in sample report, 113–114, 138–159; survey questions on, 82, 84

G

Generation X. *See* Baby busters

Generational anchors, 33

Gift acknowledgment: in sample report, 150–152; survey questions on, 85

Gift stewardship: sample guidelines on, 127–129, 163–167; survey questions on, 84–85

Globalism, 40; of baby boomlets, 40; and charitable giving, 41–42

Grants, resources on, 59

H

Hispanic Americans, demographic trends among, 31–32

I

Income and expenses: forms for, 79, 80; in sample report, 110; survey questions on, 79, 80. *See also* Budget

Individual Donors by Gift Level, by Category, and by Relationship: directions for listing, 79; sample form, 81

Individual giving: by baby boomers, 40, 41; changing priorities in, 38–40, 41–42; and increasing longevity, 30–31; personal income related to, 45; restricted, 47; stages of, 139; trends in, 27–28; in United States versus other countries, 38–39. *See also* Annual giving; Major giving; Planned giving

Information gathering. *See* Assessment survey; Environmental scanning

Interviews, 12–15; of people inside organization, 13–14, 75–77; of people outside organization, 14–15

L

Leadership: in sample report, 122–127; survey questions on, 75–77

Life stage: differences in, 37; and major giving, 47

Lifespan. *See* Longevity

Lifestyle: differences in, 37; and major giving, 47

Longevity, and individual giving, 30–31, 37

Lybnt (last year but not this year) donors, 44

M

Major giving: decrease in, 45; redefining, 45–47; resources on, 58; in sample report, 141, 143–146, 148–149; survey questions on, 86–88

Meetings: to discuss assessment findings, 11, 18–19; as information source, 51

Men, reasons for giving by, 39

Miller, P., 33

Minorities, demographic trends among, 31–33

Month-by-Month Analysis of Income and Expenses: directions for, 79; sample form, 80

N

National Charities Information Board (NCIB), 137

National Society of Fund Raising Executives (NSFRE), 54, 56

Needs. *See* Financial Needs

Nichols, J. E., 163

Not-for-profits: increasing number of, 29; resources on, 57–58, 62

O

Operating needs, 74, 109, 118

Organizational background: internal resources for researching, 51; survey questions on, 72–73

Organizational chart, in sample report, 133

P

Personal giving. *See* Individual giving

Philanthropic trends, 27–29; as environmental scan element, 25–26; in foundation and corporate giving, 28–29; increasing number of not-for-profits, 29; in individual giving, 27–28; outlook for future, 40–42; resources on, 52, 54–56; in sample report, 120–122; survey questions on, 71–72

Planned giving: resources on, 59; in sample report, 146–147, 148–149; survey questions on, 88–91; by women, 36

Program directors, survey questions for, 76–77

Projected Income and Expenses: directions for recording, 79; sample form, 79; in sample report, 110

Proposals, resources on, 59

Prospects: matching methodologies with, 44; prioritizing, 43–44, 139–140; resources on researching, 60; survey questions on, 79, 82. *See also* Donors

Public relations: in sample report, 140–141, 142; survey questions on, 97–98

R

Recognition. *See* Gift acknowledgment

Research. *See* Environmental scanning

Resources: on fundraising, 56–62; internal, 51; on national trends, 52–54; on regional and local trends, 54–56; in sample report, 162–167

Restricted giving, and fundraising among affluent, 47

Retreats, to discuss assessment findings, 11, 18–19

Ross, B., 24

S

Sample forms: Analysis of Demographic Data for Top 100 Donors, 83; Checklist for Data Collection, 64–65; Financial Needs, 74; Form for Recording Survey Information, 67–70; Fundraising History, 78; Individual Donors by Gift Level, by Category, and by Relationship, 81; Month-by-Month Analysis of Income and Expenses, 80; Projected Income and Expenses, 79; Total Prospect Pool by Category and by Relationship, 82

Sample report, 102–171; appendixes in, 167–171;

development strategy in, 113–114, 138–159; executive summary in, 106–114; introduction of, 103–106; organizational issues in, 122–138; rationale for increasing private support in, 114–122; resources in, 162–167; table of contents for, 102–103; timeline in, 160–162

Seeding, 28

70/20/10 percent rule, 43–44

Special events: declining attendance at, 38; resources on, 59–60; in sample report, 155, 158; survey questions on, 92–93

Staff: debriefing, 19; environmental scanning with, 51; interviewing, 13; organizational chart for, 133; in sample report, 112–113, 133, 138; survey questions on, 93–96

Stanley, T., 46

Stewardship. *See* Gift stewardship

Survey. *See* Assessment survey

Sybnt (some year but not this year) donors, 44

T

Taylor, M., 34, 42

Technology. *See* Computers

Time: for debriefings, 19; for development assessment process, 6, 19; for focus groups, 15; for internal interviews, 14

Timeline: for change, 23–24; for development assessment, 6, 9, 19; in sample report, 160–162

Total Prospect Pool by Category and by Relationship: directions for listing, 79; sample form, 82

Trends, value of watching, 23. *See also* Demographic trends; Philanthropic trends

V

Vice president of development: in organizational chart, 133; responsibilities of, 131

W

Wealthy, decrease in giving by, 45

Women: demographic trends among, 31, 35–36; in sample report, 119–120

World War II babies, philanthropic personality of, 34, 35, 39